KAPLAN
ADVANTAGE™

© 2011 by Kaplan, Inc.

Published by Kaplan Publishing,

a division of Kaplan, Inc.

395 Hudson Street, 4th Floor

New York, NY 10014

Permissions

Printed in the United States of America

10 9 8 7 6 5 4 3

ISBN-13: 978-1-60978-635-9

Contents

Introduction

Welcome back to school! You may be continuing with your schooling after a brief break, or you may be returning to school after many years in the workforce. Either way, we congratulate you for your commitment to improving your skills and building your career.

Higher education is tough—the work can be difficult, but that's nothing compared to the challenge of fitting all of your school commitments into your life. Many graduates look back and say that they wish they had known *how* to study when they started their higher education program. This book is designed to give you a head start—to teach you the **Academic Strategies** used by effective students now, in the first two terms of your program, so you can apply those strategies throughout your studies. In this way, you will learn more while spending less time, and that is part of the Kaplan Advantage™.

Trust your instincts

As you read this book, you will learn a series of useful strategies. They are time tested and have been used by thousands of students, but not every strategy is right for every person. You are the best judge of what works for you, and you should apply the strategies that make you the most comfortable. Studies have shown that students who work steadily over a long period of time learn more in the short term and retain more of what they learn in the long term. However, you may be a procrastinator who cannot start studying until the last minute. Many students are successful this way, despite cramming their learning into the last few hours before the test. If this describes you, then embrace your style and find a way to make it work for you—don't criticize yourself for not being a "perfect" student. There are many paths to academic success. Trust yourself, and you will find yours.

Take time to set your goals. Even if you already have a very clear sense of your goals, it will be helpful to take the time to go through the exercise of documenting them. When you review your goals and clarify them, it will help you rekindle your motivation and keep your eyes on the prize: graduation and a new career.

Survival is key. Many students think they need "A's," and they become very anxious about their grades. But remember, your goals are bigger than just one course or one grade. It may sound like a great idea to have a high grade point average, but the real goal is larger—graduation and beyond. Employers want to know that you completed your higher education program; very few will care what grade you received in any specific course. So, when the going gets tough, it's midnight before the big test or paper, and you think you are going to get a bad grade and want to quit—don't! Just get some sleep, show up, and do your best. If you keep working and ask for help when you need it, you will have your priorities in the right order. Your instructor and Program Chair or Director of Education want you to succeed and are terrific resources if you ask them for help.

Keep professionalism in mind. You have learned about the Four Pillars of Professionalism, or the EDGE: Empowered, Dependable, Goal-Oriented, and Engaged. You will be studying these concepts in depth during your Professionalism modules, but we will also remind you of them in this book. Look for the "Practice Now" features, which will give you ideas for how to improve your professionalism skills while you work on your career skills.

We are here to help

Keep this book as you work through your program. Each unit covers an important academic strategy that can be useful to you throughout your journey to success.

1. Welcome to Academic Strategies

In this unit you will learn the definition of strategy and go through a brief overview of the strategies covered in the course. In order to give you confidence in your digital sessions, we will also cover the basic parts of a computer and the most useful functions of the Internet so that you get off to a great start.

2. Goals

Everyone knows that goals are important, but it is difficult to set aside time to focus on them. In this unit, we will help you refine your goals so that they are clear and effective. We will use the SMART framework to teach you how to set and monitor your goals for the rest of your career.

3. Strengths

You are probably terrific at pointing out your weaknesses, but can you describe your strengths? It is very important to understand and access your strengths, both in your academic career and in the workplace. In this unit, we will cover the importance of strengths and how you can apply them to achieve your goals.

4. Time Management and Stress

Successful people are good at managing their time and minimizing stress. They adapt to changing situations in life and work, ensuring that they are accessing their strengths and working toward their goals. This unit covers strategies for identifying and eliminating "time wasters" so you can stay focused on your objectives.

5. Communication and Teamwork

There are some projects that you can do alone, as a sole contributor. However, most goals require cooperation with or assistance from others. This unit discusses strategic use of effective communication skills, so you can work well on teams and contribute to their success.

6. Reading Strategies

Reading is one of the best ways to learn new information. Even if you don't love reading, you are going to need to be an effective reader in order to succeed in your program, at work, and in life. If English is not your first language, or if you have a reading-related learning disability, then reading will pose extra challenges and require additional time.

But even the best readers can improve their skills. The strategies in this unit can help all readers improve their efficiency and effectiveness.

7. Note Taking

Many people take reams of notes, only to put them on the shelf, never to be read again. This unit will teach you efficient note-taking strategies so that you will find your notes useful both when it is time to study for the test and when you need them later on to review important concepts.

8. Writing Strategies

Writing is an important skill for every career. Writing is important in patients' charts, in crime scene notes, in security logs, and in construction documentation. This unit will review the critical strategies for writing clearly and cleanly so that you can communicate effectively with a variety of audiences.

9. Study Strategies

People who do well on tests follow specific strategies—and we will teach them to you. In this unit, we discuss how to apply your strengths to your studying process and how to overcome unproductive study habits. Finally, we discuss how to set up a positive study routine so that you are prepared and confident for the test.

10. Test Taking

You may be well prepared, but that doesn't necessarily mean you will do well on the test. Effective test takers maximize their probability of success by utilizing special strategies while they take tests. In this unit, we will practice those strategies so that you can show your instructor what you know.

Take control of your education

In *Academic Strategies*, you will find the keys to unlocking your best academic experience. Practice the strategies until you find the combination that works best for you. And remember, the Kaplan Advantage develops skills that are useful well beyond school—you can keep developing your strategies throughout your career and your life. You will become better at using these strategies over time, so keep the book, and review it whenever you need a reminder. You are in charge of your learning— take control of the process and make sure you make the most of this important commitment to yourself.

Acknowledgments

 hank you to the following editors for their contributions.

**Kaplan Higher Education Corporation
Chicago, Illinois**

Karen Baldeschwieler, MBA, PhD
VP, Academic Programs

Aimee Brown
VP, Marketing

Kari Costello
Executive Director, Career Services

Sarah Croft
Manager, Research and Curriculum Design

Jon Eads, PhD
Executive Director, Research and
Curriculum Design

Chakana Fowler
Director, Curriculum Operations

Yvonne Gasik
VP, Product Development

Murray Matens Kimball
Instructional Designer

Maegan K. Murphy
Executive Director, Student Experience

UNIT
1

Welcome to Academic Strategies

KEYS TO
success

Identifying the goals of this course

Describing important academic strategies

Applying academic strategies to your academic program

Identifying the basic parts of a computer, including hardware and
software

Identifying key functions of the Internet

Using the Internet effectively in your professional, academic, and
personal life

I t's shaping up to be a big year for your favorite pro basketball team. All the makings of a dream team are in place: a tall center, sharp-shooting point guards, a brilliant forward, some rising stars, and a few seasoned veterans. You watch the season opener. It's a loss. Game two comes and goes, and your team looks just plain bad. Nobody gets any steals to feed to the forward. The guards have trouble lining up three-point opportunities. The veterans don't seem to be influencing the young stars.

What's going wrong?

What your team lacks is a **strategy**—a careful plan or method designed to achieve a goal. In this case, the goal is winning games. We've all seen it happen: a sports franchise can sign the greatest individual players in the world, but without a master plan, the wins won't come. The opposite is also true. A team of B-level players can win the championship if their coach provides the right strategies.

The same concept applies to your success in school. Just like the dream team, you've got everything you need—the right courses and books, skilled instructors, and a mind that's eager to learn. But do you have a plan for using those tools? To succeed as a student, you need to follow your own set of strategies. Think of this course as your coach. It's time to make a plan.

Welcome to Academic Strategies 3

Winning Ways: Academic Strategies

This book is designed to help you put together a plan for success in your academic program. By the time you complete *Kaplan Advantage Academic Strategies*, you should be able to:

- identify strategies that help you succeed at school
- apply those strategies to your academic program, your career, and your personal life
- identify and use resources to complete academic, professional, and personal tasks
- practice effective reading and writing strategies

What Are Academic Strategies?

Academic strategies are methods or plans that help you succeed as a student. Many apply to traditional academic tasks like reading, writing, and studying. But other academic strategies are less obvious. They involve keeping yourself fine-tuned for the challenges and complexities of life as a student. For instance, methods for staying organized and communicating effectively are key academic strategies.

Why are academic strategies so important? And why should you invest valuable time learning about them? Here are just a few benefits:

They can make the difference between success and failure. Over your lifetime, your school career has probably had some highs and some lows. Here's a guarantee: at times of success, you were using academic strategies, perhaps without knowing it. And at times of failure, you were missing a strategy or two. Simply put, academic strategies work. If you use them, you will improve your grades. You will perform better on tests. And you will get more out of your education.

They keep you motivated. Having a strategy gives you direction. When you know exactly how you're going to approach an assignment, the steps are laid out for you. Without a plan, you're more likely to face obstacles or lose your momentum.

They make you more efficient. Choosing and applying academic strategies takes time, but in the end, strategies *save* you time and streamline your life. For example, you might not feel like taking five minutes to enter all of your assignment due dates in your calendar at the beginning of a course. But later on, you'll probably end up wasting a lot more time chasing after this information because you ignored a simple time-management strategy.

They help you in other areas of your life. You can apply just about any academic strategy to your professional and personal life. Do you have to pass a driving test in order to operate commercial vehicles on the job? Call on your study and test-taking strategies. Are you starting a neighborhood watch organization? Use interpersonal and writing strategies to organize your neighbors and to spread the word through a brochure.

Keep in mind that this unit is an introduction. It would take many more pages to cover all academic strategies, so we've just provided some basics. Throughout this course, you will learn about several strategies in greater detail.

Applying Personal Organization and Motivation Strategies

Our first group of academic strategies is about focusing on *you.* Part of being a successful student is keeping your mind, body, and schedule in balance. Here are some personal organization and motivation strategies, along with examples of how to apply them to your educational program:

Set goals and establish action plans to achieve them. You're in school now, so you've already set some academic and professional goals. The next step is to break down your goals into smaller tasks that you will complete within a certain time frame. This strategy will keep you motivated and give you guidance throughout your academic program.

Identify and apply your strengths and talents. Figure out what you do well, and then use your greatest assets to achieve your goals. For example, if you're a strong communicator, use your discussion skills to show your instructor how well you understand a reading assignment.

Identify and apply your learning style. Everyone learns in a unique way. For example, if you learn best by doing or performing something, carefully complete the Exercises at the end of each unit's reading. You'll maximize your academic success by catering to your style.

Manage your time wisely and set priorities. This strategy is crucial to both academic and professional success. One method is identifying and eliminating time wasters. This frees up your day for important academic tasks like reading assignments and reviewing your notes.

Manage physical health and stress. Staying healthy and minimizing stress set you up to implement all other strategies. For instance, getting enough sleep will keep you alert and attentive while studying or taking a test.

Build and maintain a strong support system. You can even be strategic about the company you keep. Spend time with people who understand the importance of your education and help you make school a priority.

TrueStory

"I went to school to become a medical billing manager. I had worked in a doctor's office before, and I thought I knew it all. I talked a lot in class but didn't listen much. During a one-on-one conference, my instructor said she appreciated my participation but thought I was dominating discussions. I took her advice and tried to spend more time listening. Some of the quieter students started talking more, and I was surprised to learn new ideas and procedures. I'm still eager to talk, but now I try to give other people air time."

Applying Interpersonal Strategies

Succeeding in school requires interacting with other people, including classmates, instructors, and other school employees. Here are a few interpersonal strategies, along with examples of how to apply them to your educational program:

Use class discussions as a learning opportunity. Don't underestimate the importance of learning from your classmates. Every instructor and student you meet has something to teach you.

Balance your speaking and listening time. The classroom is an environment of give and take. When you are in a group setting at school, remember to speak your mind, but also listen actively to others. This interpersonal strategy will communicate respect and openness.

When providing feedback, start with the positive. People are much more open to criticism if they receive some appreciation first. If you have a complaint about an assignment, or if you're responding to a classmate's idea on a discussion board, it's almost always in your favor to start out saying something positive.

When working on a team, make expectations clear up front. Success at school and at work often depends on teamwork. If you're working on a group project or presentation, write down the roles and responsibilities of each team member at the start of the project. This will keep everyone's workload fair and help you hold each other accountable.

Show openness to diversity. Schools and employers expect you to work well with people from various backgrounds. When interacting with others, express respect and appreciation for cultures, values, abilities, and ideas that differ from yours.

Applying Reading Strategies

Now we come to academic strategies that support four essential educational activities: reading, writing, studying, and test taking. These strategies will be indispensable to you throughout your schooling as well as your career. Even test-taking strategies can be applied at work— or in any setting where you experience high pressure.

The amount of written information you're required to digest in school can be intimidating. Reading strategies are methods that help you read effectively and efficiently. You'll have an opportunity to practice reading strategies later in this book. Here are a few examples:

- Before you begin reading, scan the unit's title, headings, graphics, and captions.
- Highlight important terms and topic sentences.
- Use a dictionary (print or online) to look up unfamiliar words.
- Ask questions as you read.

Apply these reading strategies whenever you read. Whether it's a textbook, your own notes from a class session, an email message from your instructor, or a technical manual at work, you will comprehend it better—and remember it longer—if you use a consistent method. This will translate into higher test scores, better grades, and job success.

Applying Writing Strategies

Writing strategies provide a game plan to follow whenever you pick up a pen or sit at a keyboard. You'll learn a lot more about writing strategies later in the book, but here's a sneak preview:

- Follow each step of the writing process: planning, drafting, revising, and editing.
- Make sure every paragraph has a topic sentence and supporting details.
- Organize every formal composition into three parts: introduction, body, and conclusion.
- Whenever you consult an online source, write down the Web address and the date you looked at the site.

Effective writing is fundamental to making a winning impression both at school and on the job. Remember that once you write something down, it can become permanent—and you can't take it back. In some cases, writing may be the only way you will ever communicate with a classmate, a co-worker, an instructor—or a potential employer. That makes it even more important to develop reliable methods for expressing your thoughts in writing.

Applying Study Strategies

Studying is a central academic activity—you simply cannot get through school without doing it! When you study, you review and master a body of information. Study strategies should *not* be limited to cramming the night before a test. Use them whenever you're about to process, share, or report on information—at a digital or classroom session, as you complete reading assignments, during a presentation, or through a writing assignment. Here is a sampling of study strategies:

- Take thorough, well-organized notes.
- Dedicate a certain place and time of day to studying without distractions.

- Organize your course materials in a way that keeps them together and makes them accessible.
- Review flashcards for key terms and concepts that you need to memorize.
- Find a reliable, hardworking study partner.

Applying Test-Taking Strategies

Tests are unavoidable if you want to achieve your academic goals. The good news is that *you* are in control of how well you do on a test. One of the least practiced test-taking strategies is to take charge of the test—don't let the test take charge of you. If you pay close attention in class and complete all assignments, you will be well prepared for the contents of a test.

Here are some other strategies that will keep you calm, cool, and successful on test day:

- Give yourself a break between studying and taking the test.
- Get a good night's sleep before the test.

- Look over the test before starting.
- Answer easy questions first, to build confidence, and then address harder ones.
- Follow up after the test so you understand your grade or score.
- When in doubt about what will appear on the test or what form it will take, *ask!*

Practice
Critical Thinking

Think of some academic strategies that have not been introduced in this unit. How have you applied these strategies in the past? How might you apply them now?

A Final Academic Strategy: Using Your Resources

Many students become caught up in solitary school activities—reading, doing research, completing writing assignments, and so on. But highly successful people excel at using *all* of the resources available to them, whether they have a specific concern or just want some general guidance. Here's a quick inventory of the types of resources you should consult:

Campus resources. Your school is organized to help *you* succeed. Call upon your instructor, classmates, program director, and Learning Resource Center.

Community resources. Check out your public library and get to know the librarians—it's their job to help you find useful information. Find out if your community has a career center. And don't forget that family members, friends, and co-workers are also great sources of information.

Electronic resources. Computers and the Internet are powerful academic tools. In the next section, we'll address some computer basics, so you'll be prepared to use electronic resources strategically.

Computer Basics

You've probably used computers many times. As you continue in school, you'll become even more familiar with them. But even some experienced computer users have trouble identifying the parts and functions of their machines. This overview of basic computer equipment will help familiarize you with an incredible tool that will assist you throughout your academic and professional career.

Nuts and Bolts: Hardware

Computer gear falls into two categories: hardware and software. We'll begin with **hardware,** which is the physical components that make up a computer. The diagrams on the next page show the main hardware components of desktop and laptop personal computers.

Here is a brief overview of each component and its function:

The **monitor** receives and displays visual information, such as graphics and words. It looks like a television screen.

You use the **keyboard** to type letters, numbers, and commands.

The **mouse** or **trackpad** is a tool that you use to interact with the computer. A mouse is a handheld device plugged into the keyboard or a port on the computer. As you move the mouse, a small arrow on the screen moves; this is the

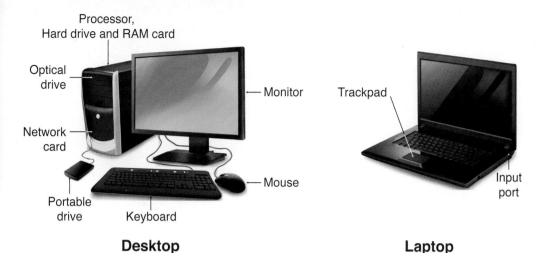

Desktop   **Laptop**

cursor. You click the button(s) on a mouse to give the computer a command. A **trackpad** has the same function as a mouse. It's a flat panel built into the keyboard of a laptop. You touch the trackpad and move your finger around on it to move the cursor on the screen. Then you click a built-in button or tap the trackpad to give the computer a command.

The **processor**—also called the central processing unit, or CPU—is the computer's brain. The processor does most of a computer's work: calculating, manipulating, and resolving data (information).

A computer has two types of memory: storage and random access. The **hard drive** is like a huge storage shed. It holds the files you create on your computer so that you can use or change them later. It also stores programs. The hard drive is located inside the computer.

Random access memory (RAM) is the second type of computer memory. Programs use this type of memory while they are running. The more RAM a computer has, the more easily and quickly multiple programs can run at the same time. You can add extra RAM to your computer by buying and installing RAM cards.

The **optical drive** is the receptacle for DVDs and CDs.

The **network card** allows your computer to connect to other computers and to the Internet.

Input ports are miniature outlets. You use them to plug in **peripherals,** or external devices that cooperate with your computer. Peripherals include printers, scanners, MP3 players, and cameras.

A **portable drive,** or external drive, is a type of peripheral. Like your hard drive, it stores files and programs. The difference is that it's meant to be mobile. You can use portable drives to back up the contents of your hard drive or to transport data from one computer to another. They are especially helpful if you use a public computer and need to take your work home.

Software

The programs, or applications, that run on a computer are called **software.** You'll probably recognize many of these basic types of software:

Operating systems. This type of software controls a computer's operations and provides a platform for other programs. Microsoft Windows® and Mac OS® are the two main operating systems used in most schools, offices, and homes today.

Word processing programs, such as Microsoft Word®, are used to create documents, such as notes, letters, reports, and essays.

Database programs, such as Microsoft Access® and FileMaker Pro®. These programs keep track of large banks of information, such as patient records at a dentist's office.

Spreadsheet programs, such as Microsoft Excel® and Quattro Pro®. People use these to make budget worksheets and other complex charts and schedules.

Presentation programs, such as Microsoft PowerPoint®.

Music and movie playback programs.

Image-viewing programs.

Internet browsers, such as Internet Explorer®, Mozilla Firefox®, and Safari®. All Internet browsers include bookmark features, also called favorites or shortcuts, which allow you to organize and easily access websites you visit frequently through a menu in the browser.

Email programs, such as Microsoft Outlook®, Mail®, and Entourage®.

Instant messaging and video chat programs, such as Windows Live Messenger®, iChat®, and Skype®.

Web applications. This type of software allows you to interact with data on a server via the Internet. Common examples are social and professional networks such as Facebook, MySpace, and LinkedIn.

The Internet: More Than a Social Network

Few inventions have revolutionized the way we work, study, and play as quickly and universally as the Internet has. One of the most influential academic strategies you can master is harnessing the power of the Internet to help you achieve your goals—and to complete countless smaller tasks along the way. The Internet is much, *much* more than a social network.

Building **Background** Feature: Internet Time Line

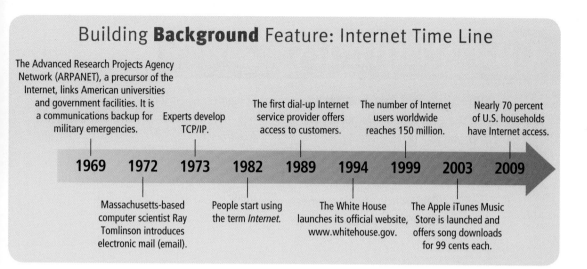

The Advanced Research Projects Agency Network (ARPANET), a precursor of the Internet, links American universities and government facilities. It is a communications backup for military emergencies.

Experts develop TCP/IP.

The first dial-up Internet service provider offers access to customers.

The number of Internet users worldwide reaches 150 million.

Nearly 70 percent of U.S. households have Internet access.

1969   1972   1973   1982   1989   1994   1999   2003   2009

Massachusetts-based computer scientist Ray Tomlinson introduces electronic mail (email).

People start using the term *Internet*.

The White House launches its official website, www.whitehouse.gov.

The Apple iTunes Music Store is launched and offers song downloads for 99 cents each.

Access the Internet

It's true that the **Internet** is a mega-network; it connects smaller networks of computers and computer facilities around the world. All of these computers and networks exchange information through a set of communication conventions called **TCP/IP** (transmission control protocol/Internet protocol). The most common way to access the Internet is to open a Web browser, such as Internet Explorer or Mozilla Firefox. You type in the address of a website, and the content appears.

Functions of the Internet

People are finding new ways to use the Internet every day. Here are some of the most common strategic uses of cyberspace in academic and professional environments:

Education: taking online courses, attending online schools and training sessions, submitting course assignments, participating in discussion boards, registering for courses, watching educational videos and lectures, checking grades

Research: finding information for research papers and other projects, using search engines, using online databases, conducting job searches, doing market research, making purchasing decisions, accessing library collections

Communication: sending and receiving email, participating in online communities, posting and viewing blogs (online journals), professional networking, chatting, instant messaging, videoconferencing

Professional tasks: booking appointments, managing calendars, charging customers, scheduling shipments, buying supplies, managing patient records, sharing and editing online documents, applying for jobs, posting resumes

Personal management and organization: keeping a calendar, managing personal finances, setting budgets

By the end of this book, your tool kit will be full. You will know about so many academic strategies that it won't be a matter of *whether* to use them, but *which* ones to employ. This is the ultimate goal of strategic thinking: being able to choose the best game plan to suit each situation.

Practice Now: Goal-Oriented

Practice being Goal-Oriented now by taking initiative. Log in to Kaplan Quad and look for the online library. Try browsing through the library and looking for articles on topics that interest you. Take the extra step to make the online library a tool that will work for you.

Unit Summary

- CS101 is designed to help you apply academic strategies to your education, your career, and your personal life.

- An academic strategy is a method or plan that helps students succeed.

- Academic strategies help you get organized, stay motivated, interact with people, read, write, study, take tests, and use academic resources.

- Computer equipment falls into two categories: hardware (physical parts) and software (programs).

- The Internet is a worldwide information network used for education, research, communication, job-related tasks, and personal organization.

Important Terms

How well do you know these terms? Look them up in the glossary if you need help remembering them.

strategy	mouse	RAM	portable drive
academic strategies	trackpad	optical drive	software
hardware	cursor	network card	Internet
monitor	processor	input port	TCP/IP
keyboard	hard drive	peripherals	

TO-DO List

✔ Write the list of CS101 goals on the first page of your notebook or computer file for this course. Revisit the goals each week and track your progress.

✔ Talk with classmates, co-workers, or friends about **academic strategies** that help or helped them succeed in school.

✔ Consult a school administrator and a public library employee about the academic and professional resources that are available to you. Gather contact information for those resources—phone numbers, email addresses, websites, and so on—and put it in a prominent place.

✔ Locate reliable sources of computers with **Internet** access. Try to identify computers that you can access at home (or close to home), at school, and at a library or media center.

Online Resources

Strategies for Academic Success: Colorado State University
www.casa.colostate.edu/Student_Achievement/Academic_Success/strategies.cfm

Learning Strategies: Maximizing Your Academic Experience
www.dartmouth.edu/~acskills/success/index.html

Introduction to Computers
www.fayette.k12.il.us/99/Intro2Comp/introduction_to_computers.html

Internet 101
www.internet101.org/

LinkedIn: professional networking and job listings
www.linkedin.com

Lynda.com: online software training
www.lynda.com

Exercises

1. Make a list of school-related tasks that have been challenging for you in the past. For each task, identify an academic strategy that will help you succeed.

2. In a notebook, write about how you plan to apply academic strategies to your chosen career.

3. Examine the computer(s) that you use for school and work. Use the diagram in this unit to identify your computer's components. If there are computer parts that are still unfamiliar to you, find an online manual for the computer model. Use the manual to identify the parts and their purposes.

4. If you have a list of bookmarks (or favorites) in your Web browser, analyze your list to determine the main ways you have been using the Internet. Then add some sites that will contribute to your academic success. For example, bookmark your school's website and the Online Resources listed at the end of this unit. If you did not have a list of bookmarks, create one now.

Goals

Defining the term *goal* and explaining why goals are important

Distinguishing between short-term, intermediate, and long-term goals

Setting SMART goals

Creating an action plan that breaks down your goals into manageable tasks

Identifying ways to stay motivated to follow your action plan

Monitoring and revisiting your goals

Identifying and overcoming barriers to achieving your goals

imagine that you're taking a long road trip to a city in another state. You've never been to this city before. About three hours into your drive, you take a wrong turn and lose your way. "No big deal," you think. You pull out your map, figure out where you are, and get back on course.

Now, imagine how this situation would play out if you had no map. You would be, literally, lost. You'd have to drive around and guess at the right path, and your lack of direction would become stressful. You'd have to rely on trial and error—or just plain luck—to reach your destination.

In life, goals are your road map to success and fulfillment. Surprisingly, many people travel through life without goals. But if you talk to successful, high-achieving people from any walk of life, you'll start hearing about their goals within minutes. Why are goals so important? Setting and keeping realistic goals are two of the most important things you can do to achieve success. Think about your career. Now that you've chosen to go back to school, you have a destination. Your educational program is like a map; it will guide you and give you motivation and focus. When you commit to well-defined goals, you give yourself direction, energy, and purpose.

It All Starts with a Goal

Let's start by looking at what a goal is. A **goal** is a specific, measurable objective that can be achieved through your own actions. It's an aim—a finish line that you strive to reach. It takes little effort to wish or dream for things to happen, but a goal is something that you take steps to achieve through effort and hard work. A goal is a dream linked to a concrete plan.

Balance Your Goals

The goal-setting techniques described in this unit can be applied to all areas of your life: professional, educational, and personal. When you set goals for yourself, try to cover a range of these categories so that your life will stay balanced. For example, if you focus only on financial goals, your family life may suffer. Finding a career that is rewarding—both financially and personally—is a powerful way to combine multiple goal categories. Job satisfaction often carries over into other areas of your life, such as health or spiritual well-being.

Practice
Critical Thinking

At lunch one day, Danisha and Vicki were talking about what they wanted out of life. Vicki wanted to get married and have three children. She thought she would be too busy raising her children to have time for school or jobs. Danisha, on the other hand, wanted to get an associate's degree, work for a couple of years and save money, and then go back to school to become a social worker. Danisha also wanted to get married and have children someday, but she wanted to have a professional career first. Which goals appeal more to you? Why?

Long-Term, Intermediate, and Short-Term Goals

The process of setting and pursuing goals in *any* area of your life can be intimidating. One thing that can make it easier is to break big goals down into smaller ones. Goals come in three sizes:

- long-term goals
- intermediate goals
- short-term goals

A **long-term goal** is big and lofty. It takes several years to accomplish—often five or more—and makes a big impact on your life. Achieving a long-term goal is a big deal. For example, your long-term career goal might be to get a job with one of the leading companies in your field. Your long-term family goal might be to get married and have three children, like Vicki in the Critical Thinking scenario on this page.

On the way to your long-term goals, you'll have to meet smaller objectives. An **intermediate goal** is a medium-size step toward a long-term goal. Reaching it is a major achievement in itself, but it takes less time to achieve than a long-term goal—often one to three years. Earning a degree or a certificate is an example of an intermediate goal. For Danisha, an intermediate goal might be earning an associate's degree.

A **short-term goal** is a small step toward achieving an intermediate or long-term goal. It may take a couple weeks, a few months, or even a year to reach. Alone it is an accomplishment, but it's also a step that gets you closer to your larger goals. Getting an A on a writing assignment is an example of a short-term goal on the way to passing a course. Saving $100 a month toward your student loans is another great short-term goal. You can think of short-term goals and intermediate goals as markers, or milestones, on the way to your greater destination.

Short-Term, Intermediate, and Long-Term Goals Work Together

It's critical to establish all three kinds of goals: short-term, intermediate, and long-term. For one thing, short-term and intermediate goals help make your long-term goals seem more attainable, because smaller steps are much less daunting. And when you know that these small steps will help you reach your bigger goal, you stay motivated to do the daily tasks that don't exactly thrill you. What if it's raining out, you're tired, and you don't want to go to your pharmacology class? It's easier to get up and head out the door if you think about how your bigger goal—becoming a certified pharmacy technician—is related to succeeding in class. When you begin to see how your daily activities can add up to something bigger, it's easier to get those little things done.

The Action Plan: Breaking Down Goals

You've already got some goals in mind—starting an academic program is evidence that you want to take your career and your education in a certain direction. Before you continue on your path, you need to know that how you state your goals matters.

Setting SMART Goals

To set yourself up for success, you need to make your goals SMART. A **SMART goal** has the following characteristics:

Specific. It's too general to use language such as "My goal is to get a job," "I want to get healthy," or "I want to learn about computers." Instead, aim for exactness: "My goal is to get a job as a network operations analyst," "I will quit smoking," or "I will pass two online courses in computer applications." It's much easier to focus on specific goals and start acting on them immediately. Vague goals disappear almost before you have the chance to act on them. If you find yourself thinking, "I don't even know where to begin," the goal probably isn't specific enough.

Measurable. A well-stated goal has a measurable end; you can put a check next to it and call it done. Let's say you want to lose some weight. How will you know when you've succeeded? If you say you want to lose ten pounds, your goal is measurable. If your life goals are not measurable, you will have difficulty knowing whether you are making progress toward them or whether you have achieved them. Always ask yourself, "How will I know when I have reached my goal?"

Attainable. An attainable goal is one that can be achieved in a reasonable manner. One easy way to check whether a goal is attainable is to determine whether other people have achieved it. For example, most students can handle working part-time while attending school, but most find it impossible to take on full-time work while in school. So, succeeding in one course at school while working part-time is probably attainable; succeeding in eight courses while working full-time is not.

Realistic. A goal is realistic if you can achieve it within the boundaries and limitations of your day-to-day life. You can start pursuing the goal right away, and you'll see clear results within a short period of time. "I will move to an apartment that is closer to my office" is probably a realistic goal. "I will move to a faraway country and get a job in my field" is probably *not* so realistic. When you dream, you don't have to worry about limits and constraints. But when you set a goal, ignoring reality can lead to failure and disappointment. Be sure to consider your specific situation; a goal that's realistic for someone else might not be realistic for you.

Timely. Every goal must come with a time frame. When will you begin, and when will you be finished? This characteristic commits you to your goal. A deadline is a signal that you're serious. Without a time frame, your chances of success decrease dramatically. For example, "I will have $1,000 in my savings account within two years" is a timely goal.

SMART goals are easier to achieve because they are well thought out. They are designed to keep you motivated, committed, and confident. SMART goals also hold you accountable; you simply can't hide from a specific, realistic goal with an established deadline. Finally, a goal that's SMART leads to an actual reward. You know when you've reached it, and you'll have something to show for it.

More Goal-Setting Tips

Here are a few more tips for effective goal setting:

Use positive language. Avoid weak or negative phrases such as "I'd like to," "I want to," "I will not," or "I won't ever." Instead, begin goals with phrases like "I will," "My goal is to," and "I am going to."

Aim for quality, not quantity. Setting goals can become addictive, especially once you start seeing results. Avoid overcommitting yourself. It's better to focus on three high-quality life goals than to juggle ten goals that wear you thin.

Research your goals. If you have any doubt about whether a goal is attainable, do some research. Ask, "Has this been done before? How often has it been done?"

What Is an Action Plan?

Once you've set some goals, it's time to come up with a specific **action plan** for achieving them. An action plan is a step-by-step outline of manageable tasks that you will complete to reach your goals over a certain time frame. It's like your GPS telling you to turn at a certain point after so many miles. Some tasks are short: "Turn left." Other tasks are long: "Drive on Route 22 for 105 miles."

Start by looking over your long-term, intermediate, and short-term goals. What do you need to do each month, or each week, to bring you closer to achieving your goals? You can think of these as "mini-goals." Then make a list of goal-related tasks you'd like to accomplish each week. Break it down even further into a daily task list.

An action plan is critical. Self-help books and websites are filled with phrases like "baby steps" and "step by step." Breaking large goals into steps *works*. It prevents you from becoming overwhelmed, discouraged, or feeling defeated. If you find yourself thinking, "I'll never get through school!" you can return to your action plan and accomplish the doable tasks of *today*: attend a two-hour class, read ten pages of your textbook, and write a paragraph in your journal. Action plans are also important because your goals are not the only commitments in your life—if only they were! Tasks related to your short-term, intermediate, and long-term goals have to fit into what may already be a complicated life. You'll be surprised at how a good time-management plan can help. Creating a schedule to keep track of your daily and weekly obligations will help you stay organized. You can choose from many different tools, from computer and smartphone calendars to traditional pencil and paper. Keep this schedule beside you as you create your action plan, and continue to make sure goal-related tasks sync successfully with your other commitments. Unit 4, Time Management and Stress, discusses many helpful tips for organizing your time and creating a schedule that will work for you.

Building **Background**

Any successful company begins—and continues to operate—with a plan. A **business plan** is a document that identifies the company's objectives, explains the reasoning behind those objectives, lists the tasks necessary to achieve those goals, and outlines the strategic plan for completing the tasks. It's the corporate version of an action plan. Should you invest in a company that doesn't have a strong business plan? Probably not. The same applies to your career: An employer is more likely to invest in you—that is, offer you a job—if you've got SMART goals and an action plan to go with them.

An action plan for any goal has the following parts:

1. **The goal itself.**
2. **A list of steps needed to complete the goal—and when you'll accomplish them.** Aim for three to five steps. For example, the goal of buying a car requires the steps of saving money, researching car models, going on test drives, and negotiating the purchase.
3. **A list of measurable tasks involved in taking each step—and when you'll complete them.** Continuing with the car example, a measurable task involved in step one would be to deposit $50 in your savings account each month.
4. **The results needed to finish each step.** For instance, you might decide to move on to researching car models once you've saved a down payment of $3,000.
5. **The date by which you intend to accomplish your goal.** No excuses on this one. Make a firm declaration: "I will buy a car by next October."

Goal Scenario One: Academic Goal

Let's look at a sample action plan for a short-term academic goal.

<u>Goal</u>

I will get an A on the final presentation for my dental radiology course.

<u>Steps and Tasks</u>

Step 1 (by Nov. 5): Research the hazards of radiation. RESULT → complete notes + citations

  – Take notes on at least six websites and two books (Nov. 2–4)

  – Make citation list with five best sources (Nov. 5)

Step 2 (by Nov. 10): Create presentation. RESULT → 12–15 notecards + 12 slides

  – Write 3-page outline (Nov. 7)

  – Write max. 15 notecards (Nov. 8–9)

  – Create 12 PowerPoint slides (Nov. 9–10)

Step 3 (by Nov. 12): Practice presentation. RESULT → Revised/final presentation

  – Deliver presentation to three people and get feedback (Nov. 11)

  – Use five best suggestions to revise notecards and slides (Nov. 12)

<u>Deadline</u>

Nov. 13: I will deliver my presentation!

Goal Scenario Two: Personal Goal

Our second example is an action plan for an intermediate personal goal. The list of tasks is abbreviated, since there are many individual tasks involved in accomplishing this goal.

<u>Goal</u>

I will run a marathon.

<u>Steps and Tasks</u>

Step 1 (by Feb. 2013): Prepare for training. RESULT —→ ready for training

- Buy running accessories and gear (Jan. 2013)
- Research different training programs (Jan. 2013)
- Prepare a new diet regimen that will supplement training (Feb. 2013)
- Create a customized weekly/monthly training schedule (Feb. 2013)

Step 2 (by Apr. 2013): Register for a marathon. RESULT —→ registered for race

- Research race dates and locations (Mar. 2013)
- Select a race based on schedule (Apr. 2013)
- Save money for cost of entrance fee (Mar.–Apr. 2013)

Step 3 (by Sept. 2013): Train for marathon. RESULT —→ ready for marathon

- Run 10–15 miles per week (May 2013)
- Run 15–20 miles per week (Jun. 2013)
- Run 20–25 miles per week (Jul. 2013)
- Run 25–30 miles per week (Aug. 2013)
- Run 30–40 miles per week (Sept. 2013)
- Prevent injuries (cross-train, rest, massage, replace shoes) (May–Sept. 2013)

Step 4 (by Oct. 2013): Run marathon. RESULT —→ race completed

- Race day! (Oct. 2013)
- Recovery (Oct. 2013)

<u>Deadline</u>

October 2013: I will run a marathon!

Tips for Staying on the Action Plan Path

If you've ever had to face a major personal challenge—like mastering a new language, quitting smoking, or losing 25 pounds—you know how important it is to stay motivated. Having an action plan in the first place is a powerful motivator, but even a roadmap can be hard to follow. The more long-term and life-changing the goal, the harder it can be to stay on track. Here are some tips for sticking to your action plan:

Write down your goals, and put them where you are forced to read them.
Always put your goals in writing. Keep a separate notebook or computer file for documenting your goals and action plans. Once you're done, surround yourself with physical reminders of your goals. Make a poster for your bedroom. Post a sign on your refrigerator. Write your goals on the first page of each school notebook. Tape a simple list to the dashboard of your car, or make it into a screen saver on your computer. In addition to posting the goal itself, write or draw your source of inspiration for the goal. It could be a person (such as your sister), an object (such as a house), or a symbol (such as a flag representing travel to another country).

Share your goals. Make your goals as public as possible. Tell your family, friends, co-workers, and acquaintances. Post your goals, as well as your progress toward reaching them, on your Facebook page or blog. Tweet about your goals on Twitter. Spreading the word about your goals will commit you to them, make them more real, and cue the people in your life to hold you accountable.

Visualize success. It's critical to divide long-term goals into smaller objectives and tasks, but *always* keep your eye on the prize. Close your eyes and actually visualize yourself having achieved your goal: driving to the office to start your new job, cooking a meal in your new house, or basking in the applause after a well-delivered presentation. When you take the time to imagine being on the other side of your goal—the victorious side—you become a magnet for miniature victories along the way.

Revise your goals. Every now and then, go back to the rules for setting goals. Do they pass the SMART test? Are your goals realistic? Focus on goals that can be achieved through your own efforts, not those that depend on things that are out of your control. Is there a logical progression from your short-term and intermediate goals to your desired outcome? Are there any unnecessary tasks on your list? Take them off. Continue to make adjustments.

Monitor your goals daily, monthly, and quarterly. Check in on your goals and your progress toward them. Every day, challenge yourself to complete tasks that will propel you toward a goal: set aside an extra hour for studying, write down a list of six or seven things you need to do the next day, or spend an extra half hour at work helping your supervisor distribute a new shipment of supplies. Each month, review your goals to make sure you are still on track. Did you accomplish everything you wanted to do? Have some tasks turned out to be easier or harder than you thought? Finally, every three months, take a step back and look at the big picture. Assess your overall progress. Are you still on track? Is there anything you can do better? Do your goals still accurately reflect what you want? Remember that your list of goals is flexible—it's meant to serve *you*.

Reward yourself. Maintaining motivation depends on anticipating some kind of reward. You will be much more likely to complete a task—especially an unpleasant one—if your mind associates it with something pleasurable or exciting. **Internal rewards** are positive feelings such as satisfaction, happiness, self-acceptance, and fulfillment. **External rewards** are tangible objects like money, material objects, prizes, compliments from friends, and other types of recognition. For every goal you set, try to pair it with at least one internal reward and one external reward. Your motivation and eventual success depend on this.

Part of Any Action Plan: A Support System

It's important to remember that in any life effort, you are not—or should not be—alone. SMART goals and carefully devised action plans aren't enough. A major part of setting yourself up to succeed is building a **support system,** or social network that helps you reach your goals. Who is there for you to support your goal and give you a pep talk when you're discouraged? Who will hold up flashcards when you're studying for a test? Who will remind you of your goal and keep it fresh in your mind?

Surround yourself with positive people and encouragement. Ask people you admire to share their success stories and give you tips. Ask your instructors how they reached their goals. Support can come from unexpected places—strangers, as well as people you already know. Find an online community of adult or nontraditional students. Start a study group at school. Join a trade organization in your industry. At the same time, wean away the naysayers in your life. There's no room in your life for people who doubt you.

Identifying and Overcoming Barriers

You've set goals and begun pursuing them, but you're not succeeding. You haven't come any closer to victory. Something isn't working. Don't despair. Just figure out what's getting in your way.

Perhaps you didn't run your goal through the SMART test thoroughly enough. Maybe your goal has been unrealistic from the beginning. What if you set your sights too high? For instance, planning to run a marathon after two weeks of training is overly ambitious. If you're guilty of over-reaching, consider revising your goal. On the other hand, maybe you never set a deadline, and time has gotten away from you. Recommit yourself to the goal by establishing a time frame and beginning your first task right away. Below are some possible obstacles, along with some suggestions for overcoming them.

Speed Bumps—Large and Small

Procrastination. Procrastination means putting something off by turning to other activities. Sometimes we lack discipline, we're surrounded by distractions, or we just have a tough time concentrating. If this happens to you, work toward your goal in an environment that allows you to focus and contains no distractions. Another technique is to figure out the ways you waste time and eliminate them. For example, if surfing the Internet is a culprit, try studying at a library and leave your computer at home.

Lack of Resources. What if you want a job in the IT industry, but you don't have the right hardware to hone your computer skills? Figure out what you need and target the most efficient way to get it. This is a barrier that your support network can help you overcome. You might know someone who can lend (or give) you a much-needed resource. You will never know until you ask.

Bad Luck. Factors beyond your control, such as sickness or a natural disaster, can completely ruin your chances of achieving a goal. Give yourself some time to focus on recovery, and then pick up where you left off. Don't dwell on the setback. At the same time, don't use bad luck as a crutch or an excuse. As Ralph Waldo Emerson said, "Every wall is a door." Sometimes what you perceive as a major obstacle can end up being a rare opportunity.

TrueStory

"When I took my first patient management course, I procrastinated so badly. I put off writing the first paper until just hours before it was due. My instructor was unimpressed when I asked for an extension. He denied it. I got an F on the paper and failed the course. My girlfriend sat me down and asked me if I really wanted to get a better job, if I was really serious. I said yes. She unhooked both of my video game players and took all my games—with my permission. I felt like I had no choice but to study. It improved my focus, and I passed the next course, and the next one, until I finished my program."

Fear. Goals represent what you want out of life, and they can help you move forward. But lofty goals usually require you to leave your comfort zone, and that can be scary. Two fears that can interfere with reaching a goal are fear of failure and fear of success. You may ask yourself, "What will happen if I fail to reach my goal?" Or you may wonder, "What if I reach my goal and it doesn't bring me the happiness or fulfillment I'm counting on?"

This is another area where a strong support system can help you. Talk with trusted friends or family members. Embrace the changes that pursuing and reaching goals will bring to your life. If you still feel paralyzed by fear, consider meeting with a therapist, social worker, or spiritual leader. Physical activities like exercise, meditation, and yoga are often helpful tools to combat fear and anxiety.

Negative Thinking. Negative illusions only serve to hold you back. The average person thinks more than 400 negative thoughts about himself or herself every day. Sometimes your brain goes into negative overdrive and you start having thoughts like, "I'm not smart enough. I can't possibly do that. I don't make enough money. I don't have enough time." These fleeting ideas may unconsciously pop into your mind, destroy self-confidence, and diminish potential.

It's important to remember that other people do not share the negative illusions you have about yourself and that those illusions do not take your gifts and talents into account. Instead of thinking about the negative, concentrate on the positive attributes that will help you achieve your goals. Build on your strengths.

Goals That Conflict with Personal Values

You're going to hit a barrier if your goals are not aligned with your personal values. **Values** are qualities and principles that are very important to you. Some examples are honesty, creativity, fairness, loyalty, and tradition. Imagine that you've set a goal to protect your children by buying a life insurance policy at the best possible price, and you're in the midst of discussing options with your uncle, who is an insurance

ON THE JOB

The structure of your workplace—or even a person you work with—might get in your way as you pursue your goals. This puts you in a difficult position because your professional and financial future might depend on keeping your job, at least in the short term. If you feel a co-worker or policy is actively preventing you from achieving a goal, consult a human resources representative or a career adviser. This person can provide concrete advice and support.

salesman. One day an acquaintance tells you that she sells insurance, and she can sell you the same plan your uncle offered you at a discounted price. You're excited about the opportunity, but you feel extremely uncomfortable. Eventually you realize that your goal to find the lowest possible price conflicts with your value of family loyalty.

If you find that you lack motivation to achieve a certain goal, ask yourself if the goal itself—or the process you're following to achieve it—conflicts with your values. You might have to revise your goal. For example, if one of your core values is environmental awareness, you could change your career goal to working at a company that is committed to recycling and other "green" practices.

On Your Way

Hopefully, several types of goals have been brewing in your mind as you've done this reading. Remember to set SMART goals, take the time to create a complete action plan, and employ strategies to stay your course. This process will have a ripple effect in both your own life and the lives of the people around you.

Unit Summary

- Goals can serve as a guide for your future and help keep you on track.

- Effective goals are SMART: specific, measurable, attainable, realistic, and timely.

- Every goal you set should have an accompanying action plan: an outline of the steps you'll take to achieve your goal in a certain time frame.

- A strong support network is critical for staying motivated as you pursue your goals.

- It's important to put your goals in writing and to evaluate your progress regularly.

- If you're having trouble reaching your goals, it helps to identify the obstacles that are getting in your way and then get the support you need.

TO-DO List

- ✔ Make a list of people and organizations that will serve as your **support system** as you pursue your **goals.**

- ✔ Write down something you did this week that provided an **external reward.**

- ✔ Write down something you did this week that provided an **internal reward.**

- ✔ Start collecting photographs or other images that represent your goals.

- ✔ Make a list of your top ten **values.** Make sure your goals are in tune with these values.

- ✔ Post your three major life goals in prominent places around your house, such as your refrigerator, your bedroom, your computer, a bulletin board, and a mirror you use often.

Important Terms

How well do you know these terms? Look them up in the glossary if you need help remembering them.

goal	SMART goal	external rewards
long-term goal	action plan	support system
intermediate goal	business plan	procrastination
short-term goal	internal rewards	values

Online Resources

LifeTango, an online collaborative goal-setting community
www.lifetango.com

GoalSetting1.com, an interactive goal-setting website
www.goalsetting1.com

myGoals.com, a website that provides goal-setting tips
www.mygoals.com

MindTools.com, a website that offers career advice, including tips for goal setting
www.mindtools.com

Exercises

1. In a notebook, write about a time when you accomplished something you set out to do. It can be something big—like graduating from high school—or something smaller, like cleaning out your closet or saving up for a trip out of town. What made you want to accomplish the goal? What specific steps did you take to do it?

2. Using the goal-setting tips discussed in this unit, come up with three long-term goals for yourself. Make sure that these goals truly reflect what you want, and make sure they fall into a variety of categories. Write down the goals in a notebook or create a computer file that you will use solely for goal-setting activities.

3. Pick a short-term goal, and write a series of daily and weekly actions that will bring you closer to that goal. Create a to-do list with *every* task you need to accomplish tomorrow, and make sure you include the actions that will support the short-term goal you've chosen.

4. Write and send an email in which you announce your goals to your family, your friends, and other members of your support network. Tell them about your goals, and provide a short version of your action plan. Ask them to help you pursue your goals in at least three specific ways.

success

Identifying your own talents and strengths

Developing your strengths through hard work and practice

Recognizing the importance of strengths diversity in a team environment

Using your unique strengths to the benefit of your team

Applying your strengths to the achievement of academic, professional, and personal goals

imagine that, in the same day, you received an A on your report card and you were in a car accident. Research has shown that you would most likely spend the next few days telling your friends and family about the negative event (the car accident), not the positive event (the good grade).[1] We have a general bias to give greater weight to negative events, objects, and personality traits. Just watch the news every night—do the anchors focus on the wonderful things going on in your community and the world, or is it all about dangers, murders, wars, and natural disasters? Unfortunately, we apply our bias toward negativity to ourselves, as well. We have a tendency to notice and amplify our negative traits—to ignore and minimize our strengths. This is not a good habit, because your strengths may be the key to your success. If you ignore them and instead focus on and obsess about your weaknesses, you are missing a golden opportunity. In this unit, you will learn how to access your strengths so you can reach your goals.

[1] Rozin, P. and Royzman, E.B. (2001). Negativity bias, negativity dominance, and contagion. *Personality and Social Psychology Review*, 5(4), 296–320.

Knowing What You Do Best

One of the keys to success is having a strong sense of self—knowing who you are. This includes identifying your talents and strengths. Knowing yourself isn't just a feel-good thing; it's an asset that will improve every aspect of your life.

Here's why it's advantageous to identify and develop your strengths:

You will achieve more. Research shows that high achievers know, develop, and apply their strengths. By playing to your strengths, you maximize your potential for success and growth.

Your confidence will grow. Focusing on your strengths—even in the process of identifying them—gets you thinking positively about yourself. It keeps you thinking about what you *can* and *will* do. Then, as you apply your strengths, other people will recognize and reward you. This relates back to the first idea: Confident people tend to succeed.

Your relationships will improve. Knowing and using your strengths will attract people to you because this shows them your best traits. It will also help you recognize and appreciate other people's unique strengths. This skill will enhance your relationships.

Your options will multiply. When you know your strengths, you learn where they can take you. Your future will begin to look boundless as your strengths broaden and deepen. Unexpected doors will open in your career, in your education, and in your personal life.

In this part of the unit, you'll explore the terms *talent* and *strength*. Along the way, you'll learn how to identify and develop your talents and strengths.

TrueStory

"When I was a kid, my father wanted me to be a policeman like him. It didn't feel like the right fit for me. He took me to the station sometimes, and I just couldn't relate to what he did. In middle school my teacher saw me always doing things with my hands—fixing pencil sharpeners, taking apart toys and putting them back together, things like that. He said I should learn about machines. My uncle was a mechanic, and I started hanging around his garage. Pretty soon if something broke down, people would get me to come fix it. Now I repair medical technology that helps save people's lives. If it weren't for that teacher, I wouldn't have developed my talent."

First Things First: Keep an Open Mind

The process of identifying your strengths is one of discovery. Surprisingly, some people live and die without ever discovering or capitalizing on their greatest talents, and most neglect to discover one or two. That's why you should pause for a moment here.

Close your eyes and visualize space opening up in your mind. Be prepared to discover talents and strengths you never knew you had.

Part of keeping an open mind is being prepared to think positively about yourself. Research into customer service (Forrester, 2009) shows that if customers have good experiences, they don't tell very many friends, but if they have bad experiences, they tell as many as they can. In today's social networking world, Blackshaw (2008) quips that "Satisfied customers tell three friends, angry customers tell 3,000!"

It's really easy to go on the Internet and write something mean without really thinking about it—or set up a petition against a company that thousands of people sign. But you shouldn't treat yourself like a dissatisfied customer, beating yourself up mercilessly for every little mistake and ignoring the good things that you do. It's hard to succeed if there's a part of you constantly setting up petitions against yourself! If you are accustomed to viewing yourself negatively, prepare for some rewiring. A positive self-image and high self-esteem are crucial to your success.

I've Got Talent

You've probably heard some variation of these comments in everyday conversation:

"You've got a way with words."

"What a computer whiz!"

"She's a natural athlete."

"He is gifted at helping people."

In these quotations, the words *way, whiz, natural,* and *gifted* refer to talent. A **talent** is a natural capability. It's an area of human endeavor that comes easily to you. Everyone is born with certain talents, which are at their service throughout their lives. Your talents are just waiting to be discovered and exercised.

To identify your talents, jog your memory. You'll remember moments when you were in a zone of excellence or accomplishment—when you were capitalizing on your talents. On the other hand, you might find that you also have a talent that has always been inside you, ready to be expressed when given a chance. For example, think about how you would complete this sentence:

If I practiced a lot, I would probably be great at _____.

Building **Background**

Self-image and *self-esteem* are two important terms in the disciplines of psychology and sociology. Your self-image is the way you perceive yourself—how you view your own body, mind, and soul. People can have an overall positive, negative, or neutral self-image. The tricky thing about self-image is that everyone holds slightly distorted mirrors in front of themselves. Those distortions can prevent you from seeing yourself clearly. And although there is no such thing as a right or wrong self-image, it is possible to have a more or less accurate one.

Self-esteem is the degree to which you value and trust yourself. It is the sum total of the opinions and judgments that you base on your self-image. Self-esteem, like self-image, is subjective—it is neither right nor wrong. But as social scientists have shown, your perceptions and beliefs about yourself can most certainly help or harm you. Self-esteem affects your emotions, decisions, actions, thoughts, attitudes, and levels of achievement and success in life.

Try to develop a positive self-image and high self-esteem. This will help you on the job, in class, and in your home life.

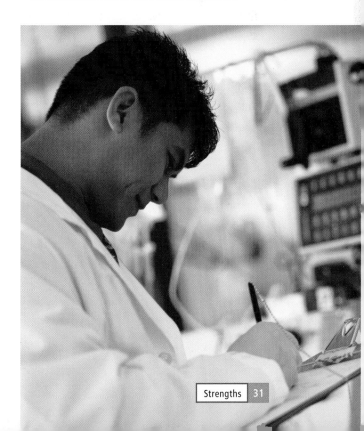

Your response to this sentence most likely reveals an area of talent that you haven't explored yet.

For more ideas, look at this list of areas of talent. Think about which areas apply to you. This is just a sample, so feel free to add more talents that apply to you.

Talent List

Music: singing, playing an instrument, composing, writing lyrics

Athletics: playing a sport, picking up sports easily, running, swimming

Communication: writing, speaking, debating

Social interaction: teamwork, resolving conflict, caring for others

Leadership: making decisions, building consensus, delegating, enlisting support, teaching

Art: painting, drawing, sculpting, decorating, crafts, fashion design

Design/construction: building, engineering, set design

Humor: telling jokes and funny stories, improvising comedic skits

Performance: acting, making presentations, dancing

Thinking and reasoning: solving problems, classifying information, recognizing patterns, making predictions, summarizing/condensing information, inventing

Cooking: baking, inventing recipes, combining flavors

Here's another approach to identifying your talents: Think back to your childhood. Summon your earliest memories and images. Visualize your childhood self fully engaged and filled with energy. What did you do? How did you spend most of your time? What activities did you return to over and over again? Which activities are similar to the tasks you face at work or in

school today? How did your childhood activities help prepare you to achieve your goals?

This exercise may help you identify your talents because children share and express their gifts very naturally. When you were a child, you had a tendency to live within your talents. Then, over time, the expectations and influences of your family, culture, and society guided you toward—or away from—certain activities and talents.

Summoning Strengths

As you continue to home in on what you do best, it's time to talk about strengths. While a talent is an innate capability that you can access with little effort, a **strength** is an ability that you have developed or mastered through practice and work. If you can do something both excellently and consistently, it is one of your strengths. For example, perhaps you can summarize an entire article or book without excluding anything important, and it happens nearly every time you read. This means one of your strengths is remembering key points in what you read. Now, what if you can throw a Frisbee with superior distance and accuracy, but it only works about half of the time? You can't quite claim Frisbee throwing as a strength—not yet, anyway. With more practice or a slight change in technique, it will come.

The good news about strengths, as opposed to talents, is that your options are endless. It is just about impossible to be talented in every area, but you can develop strengths both within and outside of your talents. Many of your strengths probably flow directly from your talents. For instance, you might capitalize on your talent in engineering by studying electrical circuits and becoming really good at troubleshooting power outages.

On the other hand, work and determination can make you strong in areas where you lack talent. You might never be a naturally gifted salesperson, but through practice and effort you can learn to present customers' options excellently and consistently. And you may not be a talented writer, but after plenty of course-work and countless assignments, you can master the art of writing professional emails and reports. If you're a disciplined person who doesn't shy away from hard work, you are way ahead of the game when it comes to developing new strengths.

To identify your strengths, ask yourself these questions:

- What are some activities or tasks that I do well nearly all the time?
- What activities or tasks have I spent a lot of time and effort trying to master?
- When authority figures such as instructors and managers evaluate me, what do they identify as my strengths?
- What kinds of rewards or recognition have I received throughout my life? For what kinds of activities or employee contributions have I been recognized? What competitions have I won or come close to winning?

Practice Now: Empowered

Empowered students are confident and communicate their strengths to other team members. If you're especially skilled at performing Internet research, or you're a strong oral presenter, be sure to let your fellow team members know this at the beginning of a group project or assignment. Focusing each team member's strengths and talents will foster efficiency and teamwork, ultimately resulting in success.

A Word About Weaknesses

With all this talk about identifying strengths, you might wonder about the importance of knowing and addressing your weaknesses. Here is another secret of high achievers: Partly because they spend so much time developing their strengths, they don't dwell on their weaknesses or deficiencies.

Focusing on your strengths doesn't mean ignoring your weaknesses. It means placing your investment where you're likely to get the greatest return. And something amazing happens when you invest your time and energy this

way. If you draw upon your talents to develop strengths in every area of your life, you'll find that your weaknesses feel, well, less weak.

If you pay close attention to yourself, you'll learn another secret: What you perceive as a personal weakness may actually be a strength in many situations. Has anyone ever accused you of being too emotional or vulnerable? How about the opposite—have you been criticized for being too distant or numb? Well, strength is in the eye of the beholder, and the beholder's opinion is also based on context. If you're a nurse assistant, the ability to sense and express emotions is an invaluable asset that could help you relate to your patients. If you're a help desk specialist, your ability to remain cool and level-headed during a network shutdown can get

Job Search **Tip**

A vital part of the job search process is being able to communicate your strengths clearly to potential employers. Get a leg up on your job search by creating a well-crafted resume that outlines your key strengths. Use strong words to highlight the areas you excel in. Are you successful at *increasing* customer satisfaction because you're a skilled problem solver? Did your strong writing skills make you a *key contributor* to a winning proposal? Powerful, precise language will project confidence and spell out to your potential employer exactly how your strengths make you a strong candidate for the job.

your company back on track as quickly as possible. So, remember that your greatest weakness is probably also your greatest strength, if you look at it from a different angle.

Summarize Your Strengths

Drumroll, please. It's time to gather your talents and strengths in one place. Review your reading and thinking, as well as the results of the thinking you've done so far in this unit. Call upon your instincts, too. Remember that a talent is a capacity that you're born with, while a strength is something specific that you can do excellently and consistently.

Now, on a piece of paper or in a document on your computer, write a list of your talents and strengths. Save this list, and revisit it regularly. Make changes whenever you wish—it will only grow!

Do you still find it difficult to write a list of your own talents and strengths? You may still feel uncomfortable viewing yourself positively; you may feel that you're bragging or being presumptuous. Remind yourself of your current goals. Remember that knowing your talents and strengths will help you achieve these goals. It's up to you.

Strength in Diversity

Imagine that you've started a new job. After a few weeks and several staff meetings, you realize that your colleagues are quite different from you. They dress differently, speak differently, and have different educational backgrounds. They make different types of suggestions during discussions. You've observed that their strengths and weaknesses are even different from yours. For example, the people on your team are very good at analyzing problems and recommending potential solutions. But when it comes to making decisions, not one of your colleagues is prepared to move forward. Promising business opportunities pass right by because everyone remains mired in the muck of too much talk.

This is where you and your strengths come in. As it turns out, your decision-making skills are incredibly strong. You understand the importance of details—the advantages and disadvantages of various options—but your strength lies in taking that final step and committing to a path. When you work on a team, remember that you've been hired for a reason.

Now that you've taken time to identify your strengths and talents, offer them up for the benefit of any team you participate in.

Strengths Diversity Defined

When you've got **diversity,** you've got variety. People most commonly discuss cultural or racial diversity, but the term applies to difference of any kind. A diverse group of people includes a variety of religions, socioeconomic and educational backgrounds, ages, ethnicities, genders, nationalities, languages, careers, physical characteristics, sexual preferences, values, capabilities, disabilities, cultural traditions, personality traits, and—you guessed it—talents and strengths. **Strengths diversity** refers to variety in the assets and competencies that people offer. This type of diversity becomes especially relevant whenever you work on a team.

Diversity is inevitable. No two people are the same, no matter how similar their backgrounds. Even people who have the same strength—such as speaking effectively and confidently in public—experience and express it in different ways. When it comes to making friends, some gravitate toward people who share their strengths, while others seek the company of those who have very different assets. But when it comes to group interaction at work, at school, and even within your own family, you often cannot choose your own teams. That's why it is crucial to know what *you* bring to a team in terms of skills, talents, and strengths. Your voice, your instincts, and your background are equally as important as anyone else's. If you don't express your own voice, your team will lack one of its most valuable assets: you.

If you're part of a team, or if you're about to join one, grasp the opportunity to contribute your strengths.

The Advantages of Strengths Diversity

Strengths diversity isn't just important, and it isn't just the right thing to do. It's an advantage. Difference may be unsettling at times, and it may even cause conflict. But conflict, when harnessed the right way, can be a source of inspiration, new ideas, and healthy revolution. You can offer something valuable to every person you meet—and that's exactly how successful people approach relationships.

Here are some advantages of strengths diversity:

It helps solve problems. People with different talents and strengths view the same problem from different angles. If everyone has the same perspective, the opportunities for breakthrough solutions are extremely limited.

It provides an immense opportunity for learning. A group of people with vastly different life experiences has a greater pool of collective knowledge than a group of people who are more similar. This pool of knowledge is a reservoir of good ideas that individuals, schools, and companies can draw from.

It increases creativity. Strengths diversity multiplies the potential accomplishments of a team immensely. Just picture a team of 34 people, each representing a different talent or strength. Every individual, including you, is applying his or her talents and strengths to the team's goals. The probability of creative inspiration becomes very high.

Diversity, in and of itself, is a strength. That's why so many schools and businesses work hard to diversify their student populations and workforces.

Maximizing Your Team Membership

Putting a diverse group of people in the same room is just the first step. Strengths diversity will not operate on autopilot. In order to take full advantage of your team's many talents and skills, you need to do your part. Be the best possible team member by following these suggestions:

Announce your own strengths and explain how they will benefit the team. Don't make people guess at your strengths. Be explicit about them.

Make sure you have a voice. If the balance of power on a team is skewed toward any one person, such as a manager or moderator, then that person's strengths may end up prevailing as well. If you feel that other team members are keeping you from exercising your strengths, bring this to your team leader's attention or find another way to express your concern.

Help identify and nurture each other's strengths. In addition to making sure the group benefits from your strengths, try to help your team members develop *their* strengths. This is one of the keys to maximizing strengths diversity.

Strengthening My Team

Start applying these tips to your own life by completing the following exercise.

Think of a team you're on right now. It can be any group of which you're a member—a course in school, a sports team, your department or team at work, a book club, and so on. On a piece of paper or in a computer document, write a list of your strengths.

Then write how you can use each strength to benefit your team.

Now answer these questions:

- What are some strengths that I may not have now, but that I could develop in order to benefit my team?
- How do the other team members' strengths benefit the group?

Applying Your Strengths to Your Goals

Now that you've done all this work to figure out what makes you shine, let's break it down and take a concrete look at how knowing yourself can help you. Imagine you want to achieve a goal—to get an A in a course, for example. In order to succeed, you must begin with a strategy, complete the coursework, and earn a top grade. Look at the chart on page 38 to see how this process plays out for two people—one who is aware of her strengths and one who is not.

When you turn the page, it will become clear who has the advantage here. Tamara's knowledge of her own strengths helps her at every junction on the path to achieving her goal. You can probably imagine the outcome if she applies this self-knowledge to her work and personal life.

Putting It All Together

And now back to *you*. You've done the work of identifying your talents and strengths, and you're ready to put them to work in a diverse environment. Now it's time to apply your strengths to achieving your key academic, professional, and personal goals.

Below are a few methods you can use to apply your strengths toward achieving your

goals. Whichever method(s) you choose, begin with the conviction that you are strong. You are strong. This can't be emphasized enough. One piece of evidence is that you have made sacrifices in order to pursue your educational goals. These sacrifices are not trivial, and most people avoid making them. So, give yourself some credit. If you recognize your own strengths, you are already partway to the finish line.

Method One: Apply Your Current Strengths

Our first method involves the strengths you know you have right now. Think of where you're comfortable and confident. Follow these steps:

1. Identify your goal.

2. From your current strengths, select one or two that are compatible with reaching your goal.

3. Call upon your skills and talents within these strengths, and apply them directly to achieving your goal.

Here's an example:

1. David's goal is to buy a house within the next two years.

2. David's strengths include listening, strategic thinking, and patience. These are valuable in helping him reach his goal.

3. David applies these strengths to the purchase of a home in the following ways:

- He carefully considers and prioritizes factors such as location, price, potential increase in home value, amount of space, home features, and versatility.
- Through interviews and careful listening, he chooses an excellent realtor, lawyer, lender, and home inspector.
- With patience, he identifies—and avoids— the risks of buying a home in an untested area, hiring a poor home inspector, and entering into an interest-only mortgage.

This method comes with a warning: Don't assume that you can or should use every last strength you have to reach a goal. Exercising all your strengths might distract you and end up compromising the goal.

Method Two: Mine Your Past

Your past successes are an incredible resource for approaching current goals. This method is very simple:

1. Recall a time when you achieved a major goal.

2. Figure out how you applied your talents and strengths to that accomplishment.

3. Replicate that process with your current goals where appropriate.

Goal Scenario: Getting an A in a Course

	Tamara: Knows Her Strengths	Ana: Doesn't Know Her Strengths
Step 1: Beginning a course	Tamara knows her strengths lie in verbal communication and bringing out the best in members of small groups. She looks at the course syllabus to find ways she can apply these strengths in the course. She sees that class discussion is an important percentage of her grade, and vows to attend every class.	Ana hasn't thought much about her skills and interests. She begins the course without strategy.
Step 2: Completing the coursework	For Tamara's course project, she has the option to write a 10-page patient report or to deliver a 20-minute multimedia presentation. She knows she is strong in public speaking but is not an excellent writer. She chooses to produce a video and give a presentation.	Ana doesn't know that she has strong listening skills but is not a particularly strong reader. She figures it's okay to miss a few lectures since she's completing all of the course reading assignments.
Step 3: Receiving an A	Tamara's participation in class discussions is excellent, and her final presentation is spectacular. She receives an A in the course.	During the final exam, Ana realizes that she doesn't remember much of the required reading. She recalls the material from the sessions she did attend, but she skipped too many lectures to pass the test. She receives a D in the course.

Here's an example:

1. Two years ago, Lydia accomplished her goal of getting a promotion from help desk specialist to desk manager.

2. Lydia reflects on her promotion. She recalls that she used her negotiation strengths by offering to take on some extra, unexpected responsibilities in the event of her promotion.

3. One of Lydia's new goals is to become a computer network specialist. She reapplies her skills by negotiating a win-win agreement with her manager: If her company pays for the training she needs, she will continue working for the company for at least two years.

Method Three: Let Your Strengths Be the Guide

In the process of applying skills to goals, the goal doesn't always have to come first. In fact, many people fail when they set goals without considering their talents and skills first. In this method, you let the talent inspire the goal. Think about what you do best, and then choose courses, activities, work environments, and jobs that jibe with your strengths and may help develop them. For example, if you are a strong leader or strategic thinker, consider running for your local school board. Or if you're good at working with your hands and you've got an analytical mind, think about the best ways to apply those strengths in your chosen career.

Practice Critical Thinking

Focusing on your talents has a potential pitfall: talent burnout. This happens when you simply do not enjoy exercising a certain talent or strength. Why do you think this happens to some people? How can people avoid talent burnout?

Again, keep an open mind about how and where to apply your strengths. Don't assume that a certain job is associated with only one strength or talent. Do you want to be a pharmacy technician? It might surprise you to know that pharmacies don't employ people with only medical or science backgrounds. Your communication, organization, and strategic thinking skills may be valuable assets.

A word of advice that applies to all three methods: Don't forget to ask for help! Career counselors, instructors, classmates, colleagues, friends, and family members are all uniquely qualified to help you achieve your goals. Take advantage of the strengths diversity inherent in the group of people that knows and cares about you. Many life goals require the effort, energy, and strengths of a village.

When Strengths Need Tweaking

What if you have identified your strengths, and you have begun applying them to achieving your life goals, but you're still not seeing the results you desire? Don't despair. Just figure out how to take better advantage of your strengths. Here are some possibilities:

You need a refresher. Maybe you're a little rusty because you haven't used a certain strength in a long time. Take a course, read an instructional manual, do some exercises, or find another way to practice. Sometimes it's just a matter of getting your mind, body, or motivation back in shape.

Consider using a different strength. When you set your goal, did you consider **all** of your strengths and talents? You might find that you're focusing on the wrong strength. For example, imagine that your manager has asked you to find a certain type of information. Instead of using your research skills to find the information online, try drawing on communication and interpersonal skills. This might lead you to people who have the exact information you seek.

Get the resources you need. What if you're missing a key piece of equipment that enables you to maximize your strength, such as a new type of dictation software or a visual aid for a presentation? Figure out what you need and target the most efficient way to get it.

Consider developing a new strength. Let's say your goal is to take a leadership position in your community service organization. The only open position is treasurer. You're excited about becoming a treasurer, but your accounting skills aren't very strong. Why not team up with the previous treasurer and learn the ropes? Why not take an online course?

Are you full of self-knowledge, bursting with talent and strength, and ready to conquer your goals? Your world is waiting.

Unit Summary

- Successful people identify, develop, and apply their talents and strengths.

- A talent is a natural capability or gift, while a strength is something that you do excellently and consistently.

- Strengths diversity is a major advantage in team environments. Groups that are diverse benefit from a wide knowledge base and a variety of perspectives and strengths.

- You can apply your strengths to the achievement of your goals by replicating past successes and allowing your strengths to guide you toward appropriate goals.

- If using a certain strength isn't leading to success, it helps to revisit your strengths and analyze how you can maximize them more effectively.

TO-DO List

✔ Call upon both internal and external sources (such as friends, relatives, and colleagues) to help you identify and confirm your **talents** and **strengths.**

✔ In the next few weeks, go out of your way to meet at least two people who are different from you and most of the people you currently spend time with. As you get to know these new people, try to share your unique strengths and try to identify theirs.

✔ Identify friends, classmates, or colleagues who thrive in diverse environments and interact comfortably with people of different backgrounds. Observe and emulate their behavior.

Important Terms

How well do you know these terms? Look them up in the glossary if you need help remembering them.

talent

strength

diversity

strengths diversity

Online Resources

StrengthsQuest, a website designed to help students gain insights into how to use their talents to achieve academic success.
www.strengthsquest.com

Clifton Strengths School, a program that teaches students how to identify their talents and integrate those talents into their academic pursuit for greater levels of personal success.
strengths.org

Society for Human Resource Management, a website serving the needs of HR professionals and advancing the interests of the HR profession.
www.shrm.org

Exercises

1. Show the Talent List on page 32 to a close friend, relative, or partner. Ask him or her for feedback about the talents you identified as yours. Did you miss any talents, either on or off the list?

2. Show the Strengthening My Team exercise on page 37 to another member of your team. Discuss the various strengths of all team members. Come up with a plan for taking advantage of your team's diverse strengths.

3. Find a manager, colleague, instructor, or friend who shares at least one of your talents or strengths. Interview the person about how he or she applies his or her talents and strengths to achieving life goals.

4. Revisit the three goals you wrote at the beginning of this unit. Write an action plan detailing how you will use your strengths to achieve each goal. Use one or more of the methods proposed in this unit.

UNIT
4

Time Management and Stress

success

have you ever wondered what the difference is between athletes who make the Olympic team and those last few to be cut? You might think the ones who make the team are more talented or train harder. However, research shows that all world-class athletes have about the same level of talent and train with the same intensity. The ones who reach the top are actually those who are better at rest and recovery from the intense stress of their sports.[1] If you want to be an academic champion, you, like a world-class athlete, must learn to manage stress. In this unit, you will learn strategies for using your time wisely in order to keep stress from coming between you and your goals.

[1] Loehr, J. (1995) *The New Toughness Training for Sports: Mental Emotional Physical Conditioning from One of the World's Premier Sports Psychologists.*

Defining Stress

You probably have heard a friend, relative, or co-worker say, "I'm so stressed out!" Maybe you've even used that common phrase yourself. But what does it mean? When people claim to be "stressed out," or under **stress,** they usually mean that they feel like their lives are out of control. They have too much to do and can't get it all done, or they have problems that they cannot easily resolve.

Engineers use the term *stress* to refer to pressure that is applied to materials or objects. If a material is stressed to the point of failure, it breaks. You can see how that is similar to the way we commonly think of stress in our lives. We feel emotional pressure when things don't seem to be going well or when we have too many responsibilities. The pressure might cause our performance to suffer or even cause us to fail at certain tasks.

Doctors and psychologists define *stress* even more specifically. We place many demands on ourselves every day, mentally, emotionally, and physically. Our bodies respond to all these demands, not just the physical ones. If the demands are too many, or too intense, our bodies regard them as a threat and cannot adequately respond. The body's inability to respond to perceived threats, whether they are real or imagined, is the clinical definition of stress.

Signs of Stress

Stress has many symptoms, or signs. Signs of stress can appear in your physical health, your mood, and your cognitive performance, or your ability to think and learn. In turn, physical, emotional, and cognitive challenges affect behavior. These are some common physical symptoms of stress:

- headaches
- muscle tension and pain
- chest pain
- fatigue
- upset stomach
- sleep problems

Often the discomfort from these unpleasant physical effects of stress causes us further stress, creating a never-ending cycle of stress.

Stress also produces emotional symptoms that affect mood. Common mood-related signs of stress include:

- anxiety
- lack of motivation
- restlessness
- irritability
- sadness
- depression

Stress can cause an inability to focus and concentrate, as well. Procrastination and nervous habits, such as nail biting and pacing, are behaviors that can result from these mental symptoms of stress. As with the physical signs of stress, cognitive and mood-related effects can contribute to an ongoing cycle. If we are unable to focus or don't feel up to doing the things we need to do, responsibilities can pile up around us and cause—you guessed it—more stress!

Causes of Stress

Life is demanding. Every day we are challenged to meet a long list of needs and expectations for others and ourselves. Working and paying bills, taking care of family and friends, eating right and exercising—the list goes on and on. But what is the difference between an ordinary busy day in an active life and a stressful day? Which activities are a part of a normal routine and which ones are stressors? The answer is, "It depends." A **stressor** is any factor that causes an organism stress. As individual human beings, we are different. A factor that causes one person stress may not affect another person at all.

Stressors can be environmental conditions such as annoying noise, daily events such as traffic jams, or significant life changes such as divorce or job loss. Stressors may be brief or ongoing, but those that are ongoing or cause a lasting change are the ones that affect our lives the most. The strain of caring for an elderly parent, paying for the expense of childcare, or dealing with a sudden loss of income after a partner is laid off from a job are examples of significant stressors. Situations such as these are not easily or rapidly resolved.

Stress is certainly a part of life for an adult student returning to school. In fact, many adult students have a number of stressors to overcome in order to succeed in their academic programs. The U.S. Department of Education identifies seven risk factors that make it more challenging for people to graduate from a postsecondary institution. Most adult students have one or more of these risk factors that can be stressors:

- Did not graduate from high school
- Started college after age 19
- Attends school part-time
- Is financially self-supporting
- Has dependents to support
- Is a single parent
- Works full-time

Do any of the items on this list describe you? If so, give yourself some credit for overcoming challenges and making sacrifices to pursue your education.

Building **Background**

How do we describe ourselves?

Physically We have physical bodies.

Emotionally We have feelings.

Cognitively We think and reason.

Behaviorally We act.

These categories help us organize our ideas about ourselves, but we are whole people. Factors that affect us in one area really affect us in all areas. How we feel physically affects how we feel emotionally; how we feel emotionally influences our thoughts and our ability to concentrate. What we think and feel determines the way we behave. Our behavior affects our interactions and relationships with others.

Positive Stress

From what you have read so far, it would be easy to conclude that stress is entirely negative. This is not the case. Most people actually work better under some pressure. **Positive stress** occurs in situations in which, under the right amount of pressure, a person's performance improves. You might have faced a tough situation and found you were not only able to handle it, but handled it very successfully. Pressure that produces positive stress causes you to perform well and yields positive results.

So, if positive stress leads to success, then no stress at all must lead to even greater results, right? Not true. The opposite of positive stress, **negative stress** occurs in low-pressure situations, often leading to boredom, loss of focus, and low performance. In situations with no pressure, there is little incentive or motivation to perform well. For example, if there were no test at the end of your course, do you think you would put the same amount of work into studying? Probably not. And if you didn't apply yourself to the work, you wouldn't learn as much. Obviously, then, it is better to identify your **optimum stress** level—the ideal pressure that prompts you to give your best performance. An individual's performance begins to suffer if pressure rises beyond his or her optimum stress level. So, focus on finding exactly the right balance for you. Stress works the same

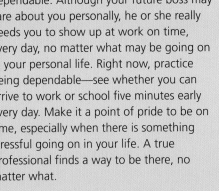

Practice Now: Dependable

Practice Now: Dependable

Employers want employees who are dependable. Although your future boss may care about you personally, he or she really needs you to show up at work on time, every day, no matter what may be going on in your personal life. Right now, practice being dependable—see whether you can arrive to work or school five minutes early every day. Make it a point of pride to be on time, especially when there is something stressful going on in your life. A true professional finds a way to be there, no matter what.

way—individuals experience stress differently, and stress responses vary from person to person, so you need to find a stress level that is just right for you.

Stress and Professionalism

We can't avoid stress. And working professionals and serious students have more stress to manage than usual—by choice! People who set professional and academic goals for themselves accept that they will have to meet additional demands to achieve those goals. Professionals put themselves in situations in which they must manage high levels of stress, in hopes of achieving promotion and the benefits that come with advancement. Students engage in a similar trade-off in pursuit of graduation. In order to achieve ambitious goals, you must find a way to perform effectively, regardless of the stressors.

Type of stress	Positive stress	Negative stress	Optimum stress
Amount of stress	High	No or low pressure	Positive pressure
Performance	Increases	Decreases	Increases greatly

Many people find work stressful. In order to meet their goals and stay in business, companies apply pressures, such as expected workloads, incentives, and deadlines. Ideally, work stressors produce the optimum stress level to encourage employees to perform at their best. In reality, however, employees are people with complex lives. They also face personal stressors relating to family, finances, and health. The combination of personal and professional stressors can add up. Almost every working adult feels, at least some of the time, as if he or she has too much to do and too little time in which to do it.

TrueStory

"I'm a Medical Office Specialist in a very busy doctor's office, so I'm the person people call when they have a problem with a bill. One patient called and was very upset about a bill she said she had paid. I heard a screaming baby in the background. When I politely explained to her that I would need a few minutes to look up her account, the woman began yelling at me. I was very upset, too, as I listened to her. But then she said, "I'm sorry. I didn't mean to be rude. Last night was really rough. If you only knew what I've been through." I reminded myself that you never know what another person is dealing with."

Managing Stress

It seems logical that the best way to reduce stress is eliminate stressors. But eliminating stressors does not necessarily remove stress. New stressors may take their place. For example, you might decide that you have had enough of the stressors of a particular job. However, if you leave that job, you take on the new stressors associated with paying the bills while you find a new job. The stressors associated with school may tempt you not to complete your education. But if you leave school, you will probably face the stressors that led you to enroll in the first place. And some ongoing stressors, such as caring for the special needs of a loved one, simply cannot be removed. We cannot eliminate stress from our lives, but we can manage stress in order to be at our healthiest, happiest, and most productive.

How Can You Reduce Stress?

There are several strategies that can be used every day to reduce and manage stress in each part of your life.

Schedule Recovery Time. Remember those Olympic athletes you read about at the beginning of the unit? Their exceptional performance is credited not only to talent and training but also to the ability to recover from the demands of their sports. Like them, you can regain and improve your ability to perform by giving yourself proper time to recover from the strain exerted by stressors in your life. It may seem like scheduling recovery time in an already busy schedule would lengthen your "to do" list—and add more stress. But scheduling recovery time is an investment that pays off.

Getting the proper amount of rest is important to recovery, and there is ample research on the amount of sleep that people need to stay healthy. Adults generally need seven to nine hours of sleep per night. How much sleep is

right for an individual depends on factors such as age and the quality of sleep. A person whose sleep is frequently interrupted or cut short will need more. Sleep is not the only type of "rest" that helps you recover from stress, though. Taking an active break from the stressors in your life also helps, and scheduling time to do so is important.

One of the best ways to manage stress is to make sure you have something each day that you look forward to. Regular vacations to a tropical paradise would certainly be nice! But looking forward to something small every day is equally effective at helping manage stress. Do you know someone who starts his or her morning routine by doing the newspaper crossword puzzle over coffee? For a busy person, that ritual can be like a regular morning "mental vacation" and serve as a helpful stress reducer. For a pet lover, walking the dog each day after dinner can provide a similar break. Or, take a peaceful walk by yourself, or just watch your favorite TV show. Your recovery time does not need to be long or involved—it just needs to be something that you enjoy.

Of course, if you schedule recovery time in a way that deters you from meeting important obligations, you'll really just add to your stress level in the long run. Which leads us to the next tip—organizing.

Get Organized. Reducing stress first requires that you organize your stressors. How can you organize stress when everything must get done? Remember that your obligations do not all hold equal importance. In other words, not everything on your to-do list must be done at once. Give some thought to the order of importance of the demands in your life. Making a list can help you prioritize each item by importance. For example, you have a big test tomorrow and you also need to get new shoes for your daughter. You might decide that studying is more important and plan another day to shop. If you know which obligations are the most important, you can plan to accomplish those first. You most likely will experience a sense of relief. Getting the "big stuff" done reduces stress—in a big way.

Practice. Another habit that helps reduce stress is practice. Practice doesn't always make perfect, but it does make *better*. If you practice performing a high-stress task when the pressure is not actually on, you can prepare yourself to perform better when the pressure *is* on. Suppose, for example, your supervisor asks you to give a status report in the staff meeting on Mondays. You've never had to speak in front of your co-workers before, and the thought makes you very nervous. Practicing at home can help calm your nerves and prepare you for the staff meeting. The more you are able to practice performing high-stress tasks, the more you can clearly identify your challenges and develop plans to deal with them. Then, you will be ready to approach those tasks with a can-do attitude under reduced stress.

Plan. Having a backup plan is also a good way to reduce stress in your life. Most of our days are planned out to the minute, and one change can ruin the whole day. But not if you have a backup plan. For example, say your mother watches your children while you are in school. This week, however, your mother has the flu. She is too sick to babysit, and you don't want your children getting sick, anyway. If you have a plan B—your neighbor has offered to watch your kids, or your sister is available sometimes—you don't need to be stressed about not having your regular childcare. Or maybe you know that your car can be unreliable, leaving you without a way to get to work. Mapping out public transportation in preparation for days when your car won't start reduces stress and helps you get to work on time.

Finally, having a positive attitude goes a long way when it comes to reducing stress. Things won't go smoothly every day—you will be late, forget something important at home, feel tired. But choosing to laugh at the stressors in your life can make you feel less stressed.

Dealing with Stress

An awareness of the stressors in our lives is our first step in reducing stress. We can also use physical and mental relaxation strategies to help us deal with stress factors that we cannot reduce. Relaxation strategies can help reduce the effects of stress such as anxiety, tension, and fatigue, to name a few.

When you think of physical relaxation, you might instantly picture lounging under an umbrella in that tropical vacation paradise. Physical relaxation can also be intensely active, though. Vigorous exercise, such as running, weight training, or competitive contact sports, leave many people feeling both relaxed and energized. These can be great ways to overcome the muscle tension, restlessness, and lack of motivation that are symptoms of stress.

Other physical relaxation strategies are, indeed, quiet and still. Breathing techniques can help a stressed person feel more relaxed very quickly and can be performed at almost any time and place. Think about how you breathe when you are relaxed or just before you fall asleep. Your breathing at those times tends to be slow and fairly deep. Deep breathing sends a message to your brain to slow down and can help

you relax. You can do it anywhere, anytime, and nobody else has to know that you are doing something to manage stress. Try it now. From your abdomen, breathe in for four slow counts, and then breathe out for four slow counts. Close your eyes and repeat the process four times. Yoga is another effective means of physical relaxation. It involves moving the body through a series of poses, combined with deep, controlled breathing.

Mental relaxation strategies can also help us deal with symptoms of stress. Meditation is the practice of training one's mind to self-start a state of relaxation. Though it may sound simple, it can be challenging for a person with a lot on his or her mind to focus deeply on a single thought and become "mentally still." Guided imagery can be a helpful relaxation technique for such people. Guided imagery is a series of directed thoughts, usually involving visualization. A guide, in a soothing voice, describes the sights, sounds, and smells of a pleasant setting, leading the listener to mentally "go to that place," away from life's stressors. Progressive muscle relaxation is another technique in which a person, with or without a guide's voice, consciously relaxes one muscle at a time until the entire body is free of muscle tension. You can find many audio recordings for guided imagery and progressive muscle relaxation online.

Meditation, guided imagery, and progressive muscle relaxation are very deliberate mental relaxation strategies. Simple hobbies that bring pleasure and provide a temporary escape can also counteract the effects of stress. Art, sewing, cooking, music, movies, gardening, and reading are a few examples of hobbies that help people relax. Have you ever heard the saying "Laughter is the best medicine" or the phrase "comic relief"? Laughing with friends or at a funny movie is not only a good time; it's also a great stress reliever!

Find a Balance

Everyone's life includes at least some stressors. And every person can take steps to manage and reduce stress in his or her daily routine. **Chronic stress** occurs, though, with exposure to difficult circumstances over a prolonged period of time. The body has built-in responses for perceived threats. Under chronic stress, the body doesn't get a chance to enter the relaxation state it needs for rest and recovery. The "always on" mode can have serious negative effects on the body. Chronic stress can significantly damage both physical and mental health, contributing to countless diseases as well as severe depression.

Stress can be dangerous, but if you can't eliminate it from your life, what *can* you do to stay well? First, you can equip your body to better handle stress by eating well and getting appropriate amounts of sleep and exercise. The healthier you are to begin with, the better your body will perform through trying times.

Next, you should find your optimum stress level and know when you are exceeding it. Be aware of the signs of stress, and recognize when home, school, and workplace stressors have accumulated to the point that you are showing stress symptoms. In the next section of this unit, you'll read about ways to prioritize and manage your time to best meet demands and cut down on stress.

Finally, know that you are not alone in feeling stress, nor is "going it alone" the best way to deal with stress. A family member who can babysit for an hour, a friend who can drop off some groceries, a co-worker who can trade a shift, and a classmate who can be a study partner—all can make a big difference during a stressful time. Creating a support network of people you can count on for help in a pinch, and helping in return whenever you can, is a powerful way to keep stress under control.

Prioritizing

You've read that the demands we face become stressors when our bodies interpret those demands, real or imagined, as a threat. So, if losing your keys on a busy morning is a stressor, is it accurate to say that your body is threatened by missing keys? Well, not really. The threat comes from feeling as if you are going to fail at something important because you already had a different expectation to meet during the time you now must use to find your keys.

So much to do, so little time. Nearly every moment of our lives is booked up. And life also has a way of surprising us with extra problems when we have the least time to solve them. What if something doesn't get done? Examining your priorities and asking, "So what?" will help you figure out whether those threatening failures that you perceive really matter.

Take Control of Your Time

There are only 24 hours in a day—no exceptions! Your decisions about how to spend that time make a significant difference in your stress level, your performance, and your quality of life. Some demands on your time are nonnegotiable. You have to be at work or in class at specific times. You may have little or no control over how many or which of your hours are occupied by work and school. Though you have some control over when you sleep, the amount of time you need to sleep is also nonnegotiable. Your body needs the amount of sleep that it needs, and if you deprive it, your body, mood, and mind will be negatively affected.

Most people would agree that a quality lifestyle must consist of more than work, school, and sleep. In fact, most of our lives demand more than work, school, and sleep. We have families and homes, friends and commitments, goals and dreams. Our days become a series of tasks. We are often forced to differentiate between accomplishing the tasks we *need* to and accomplishing the tasks we *want* to. Some tasks don't make the cut, and some goals go unmet or get postponed. Personal obligations can prevent us from accomplishing goals as quickly as we had hoped.

We have to be realistic about the time it takes to get things done and about which tasks really help us achieve our goals. It is important not to let go of all our wants while we are addressing nonnegotiable needs, but we do need to set each task as a **priority,** or as something important. Prioritizing is assigning a level of importance to a task. Higher-priority tasks are completed before lower-priority ones.

Setting Priorities

Think about the elements of your life that are really important. What do you need in life? What do you want? What can you honestly do without? In order to set priorities, you must assign some rank to your needs and wants. Of course, basic needs like food and shelter rank highest on every person's list. But after the basic needs are met, people's needs vary dramatically. Think about what makes you happy, what makes you sad, what makes you nervous, what makes you feel secure, what makes you frustrated, what makes you feel accomplished. What enables you to be at your best? What causes you to make mistakes?

Considering what you need from life in relation to what you want, and ranking your needs and wants in order of importance, will help you prioritize how to spend your valuable time. Spending your time wisely is an important behavior for minimizing stress in a busy life. Again, the basic needs of food and shelter dictate that performing well at a job, because of the income it provides, is one of those nonnegotiable uses of time. Work climbs high on the priority list.

You might be a person who favors a tidy environment and is most comfortable when all the floors in your home are swept. Unlike your work schedule, over which you probably have little control, sweeping your floors can be put off with little consequence. That priority can fall toward the bottom of the list. It is a task that still needs to be done eventually, but it can be postponed without becoming significantly harder or more time-consuming.

Some tasks may not be urgent, but when postponed they become more difficult, so putting them off until later does not pay off in stress reduction. For example, you might not get around to organizing your bills one month. A month later, you have twice as many bills to account for and have had twice as long to lose track of receipts. It becomes harder to be certain your records are accurate, and you probably have to go over everything more than once. If you forget to pay a bill, you could be charged fees that become a new financial stressor. Regularly organizing your bills should probably rank higher on your priority list than sweeping your floors.

Deadlines also dictate priorities. Although some tasks get more difficult if they are postponed, other tasks become impossible if they are not completed by a certain time. School courses have firm enrollment dates. Homework assignments have due dates. Tasks that need to be completed by a deadline rise in rank on the priority list as their deadlines approach.

Some tasks are short and easy, but other tasks take a long time (and maybe a quiet environment) to complete. It is easy to focus on the short and easy tasks and finish them quickly and never get to the longer and more difficult tasks. This can become a stressor when the deadline for the longer task suddenly arrives, and you don't have enough time to complete it. When you are making your priorities, set aside time for longer tasks or tasks that require quiet or uninterrupted time.

With work, home, and school tasks competing for rank on your priority list, it is common for personal priorities to get pushed to the bottom of the list. As you read in the unit on goals, personal goals can be postponed indefinitely until they fade into distant memory as long-lost wishes. Try to remember that prioritization is a strategy for reducing stress and improving the quality of your life. If all the priorities on your list relate to needs and none relate to wants—if none of the priorities on your list relate to relaxation and recovery—you probably have room to improve your stress management strategy. Feelings of regret are nonproductive, and yes, stressful! Assess personal priorities according to how much you will regret *not* doing something before you let it continually slide down your list and drop off entirely.

Creating a Time Management Plan

Ranking your priorities on a list can help you determine how you should spend your time, but how do you *actually* spend your time? You might be surprised at how far the real differs from the ideal. To develop a time management plan, you must first take an honest look at how you spend your time and determine whether you have any habits that you need to change.

Assess Your Habits

Have you ever gotten to the end of a busy day, felt like you didn't get much done, and asked yourself, "Where did the time go?" Demands of our daily routine add up, and we spend hours doing things that we can't tie directly to the accomplishment of our goals. To learn whether you have habits that are working against you, keep a detailed record of how you spend your time over the course of a few typical days. Make a table to help you track your observations quickly so you don't spend all your time recording notes about how you spend your time (see Figure 4.1).

Monday	Tuesday
6:30–8:00 get ready for work	6:30–7:15 get ready for work
8:00–9:00 commute to work	7:15–7:45 practice for quiz
9:00–9:45 talk to co-workers	8:00–9:00 commute to work
10:00–11:40 prepare paperwork	9:00–11:50 prepare paperwork
12:00–1:00 lunch with friends	12:00–1:10 lunch with friends
1:00–1:40 check emails	1:15–4:50 finish paperwork
2:00–4:40 finish paperwork	5:00–5:45 drive home
5:00–5:40 drive to school	6:00–6:40 digital session work
6:00–8:40 class	7:00–8:40 made and had dinner
9:00–9:40 drive home	9:00–10:00 digital session work
10:00–11:00 watch news	10:00-11:00 flash cards
11:00–11:40 check Internet sites	11:00–11:15 check Internet sites
11:45 bed	11:15 bed

Figure 4.1 Sample time log

After you've completed a few time logs, analyze your observations. What do you spend your biggest blocks of time on? A long time block is an extended period of time spent on a designated priority, such as an entire workday. Was the progress you made during your long time blocks worth the time spent on task? Long time blocks don't always produce the desired progress compared to the time on task. It is easy to let distractions cause big tasks in long time blocks to take more time than they should.

Which activities on your time logs do not contribute to your achieving important goals, and how much total time did you spend on those activities? Many of our routine habits are time wasters. Common time wasters include watching TV, playing video games, surfing the Web, interacting through social networks, texting, and talking on the phone. If you text routinely throughout the day, it may seem like no big deal to spend five minutes in an hour to stay caught up with friends. But totaled over the typical number of waking hours in a day, you might easily find you are spending nearly an hour and a half texting every day, seven days a week. An hour in front of the TV and 15 minutes a day on a social networking site add up to almost another ten hours! What priorities on your list could you address more effectively with an extra 20 hours in your week?

It is tempting to fit trivial activities such as texting into gaps in our workday, or time when we have to wait between one "official" task and the next. Part of using time efficiently is identifying gaps and filling them with numerous small tasks that can be accomplished during the otherwise idle time. Having a prioritized list of tasks can help you be ready to tackle the smaller but still important tasks when gaps present an opportunity.

Build a Schedule

If you look at a log of how you spent your time in a given day, you will see that you spent time

on many tasks that you needed to complete. You also spent time doing other things that you didn't need to do. Were those things a waste of time? That depends on whether you got your important tasks done first. To help you stay focused and make better use of your time for the day ahead, you can prepare a task list. A **task list** is the list of all the tasks an individual needs to accomplish in a day. If you use a task list, and check off the items you need to get done as you complete them, it can help motivate you to get

To do list

- Read book assignment
- ~~Pay rent~~
- ~~Sign up for spring classes~~
- Check auto insurance policy
- Talk to study group — what day to study

through the necessary tasks more quickly, so you have some free time at the end.

A task list that assigns tasks to specific blocks of time in your day is a schedule. It's very common in the workplace to have a clearly defined schedule that allocates time for specific tasks. It is less common for people to schedule their personal time. However, if you are feeling regular stress over having too much to do and not enough time to do it all, preparing a schedule can be a big help. Schedules allow you to budget time, balance activities, recognize when you are planning too much, and organize your days more efficiently.

You have ranked your priorities on a list, and you've observed how you actually spend your time. Now make a schedule that shows the time slots you have reserved to complete your different priorities. Draw a grid and fill out your tasks and goals for the day and week. (See figure 4.2.)

Be sure your schedule includes all your hard obligations. A **hard obligation** is a task or commitment with a specific time frame or deadline. These are the most important tasks to place on your schedule so that you address them on time. **Soft obligations** are tasks or commitments without a specific time frame or deadline. It is important to write soft obligations on your schedule so you don't overlook them.

Tools for Time Management

You might not have time to make a detailed schedule to outline every task you need to complete during each day. There are many time management tools you can use, though, to

Monday	
6:00	Exercise 20 minutes Get ready for work
7:00	Eat breakfast with kids
8:00	Commute
9:00	Complete paperwork due today; organize paperwork for afternoon
10:00	
11:00	
12:00	Lunch with friends Plan homework
1:00	Complete paperwork due end of day
2:00	
3:00	Quick break (20 minutes) Finish paperwork
4:00	Meet with supervisor about new computer system
5:00	Drive to class
6:00	Class
Evening	Review assignment before bed; go to bed at 11:00

Figure 4.2 Sample schedule

remind you that your most important tasks are due. Reminders can keep you on track to complete tasks on time. Most cell phones, even simple models, now have calendars on which you can place event reminders. Smart phones have more complex scheduling applications that can track appointments, hold detailed notes, and sync with schedule programs on a computer.

Cell phone capabilities are now broad enough to enable them to take the place of PDAs, personal digital assistants. A PDA is a portable, handheld electronic device that can hold a great deal of information, like a computer. Organizing your time does not require digital technology, however. A small paper notepad or stack of index cards can provide equally portable and effective reminders of appointments and deadlines.

Computer programs that help with scheduling and time management are too numerous to count. From basic printable calendars to customizable calendars that you can share online, time management tools are among the key benefits of the personal computer. You can set reminder timers in most email programs to show you an alert before you have something due. Or you can use a spreadsheet program to develop a step-by-step schedule of all the work tasks for an entire project.

Whether you prefer computer technology or paper time management tools, listing your tasks, scheduling time for them, and monitoring your progress against the schedule will help you work more efficiently.

Making Choices

All the scheduling and planning in the world will not permit you to complete 20 hours worth of tasks within the 16 waking hours of a day.

Time is, quite simply, a limiting factor. After you have analyzed, prioritized, and scheduled your time, you will often find you need to cut some tasks from your list. Some lower-priority goals must be sacrificed in order for you to achieve the more important goals. Making those sacrifices will likely be a bit stressful; but not achieving important goals because you are spread too thin will be significantly more stressful.

As you make these choices, many of them tough, you may need to spend less time with some people. You will have to practice assertiveness and the willingness to say *no* to distractions so that you can accomplish tasks related to important goals on time. You'll need to explain your choices to friends and family so they understand why you might need to decline an invitation or cut a visit short.

If you plan tasks as far in advance as possible and work on big projects in short, regular increments, you can make more compromises and fewer outright sacrifices. No matter what, meeting deadlines reliably is a must for professional and academic success.

Practice
Critical Thinking

Scheduling your time effectively involves more than listing tasks in time slots. That's a start, but you can also give more thought to which tasks are best completed at which times. Suppose, for example, you have a 20-page chapter to read for school and it's due in four days. You might plan to read the whole chapter the night before class, hoping that you're not too tired and that nothing unexpected comes up. Or, you could plan to read five pages each day on your lunch break when you are more alert. If you are at your sharpest in the morning, you might read part of the chapter in the morning instead of spending that time on the newspaper. You can shift your newspaper reading to lunchtime or bedtime. Scheduling time to do important things is only part of skilled time management. Think about ways to break apart big, important tasks and approach them when you are at your best.

Unit Summary

- Stress is the body's response to a perceived threat, real or imagined; the effects of stress can be physical, emotional, cognitive, and behavioral.

- Stressors can be physical or emotional demands, environmental conditions, and routine or extraordinary circumstances.

- Much of our stress comes from feeling like we have too much to do and not enough time to do it.

- Prioritization can help us decide which tasks are worthy of our time.

- Active time management helps reduce stress and improve performance.

Important Terms

How well do you know these terms? Look them up in the glossary if you need help remembering them.

stress

stressor

positive stress

negative stress

optimum stress

chronic stress

priority

task list

hard obligation

soft obligation

Exercises

1. Consider the effects of stress. Imagine that you are running late for a very important class or work meeting. You run into the class or meeting over 15 minutes late. What effects might you notice physically, emotionally, cognitively, and behaviorally? Make a chart that lists how you might feel and act at the meeting.

2. Think about a typical weekday and record all of the stressors in your day. Then rate each stressor as positive, negative, or optimal, and list its effect on your goals. Plan ways you can turn positive and negative stress into optimal stress.

3. Create a list of everything you need to do for the week. Then create a list of everything you want to do this week. Compare both lists and plan how you can schedule your wants in with your needs every day, making time for recovery. Make sure to consider obligations that must be done and tasks that are less important.

4. Record how you spend your time each day for a week. Then review the time management strategies given in the unit and choose one or two that will work in your life. Create a schedule using one of the time management systems, being sure to consider your goals as you plot time for each task. Follow the schedule for a week and then make changes as needed.

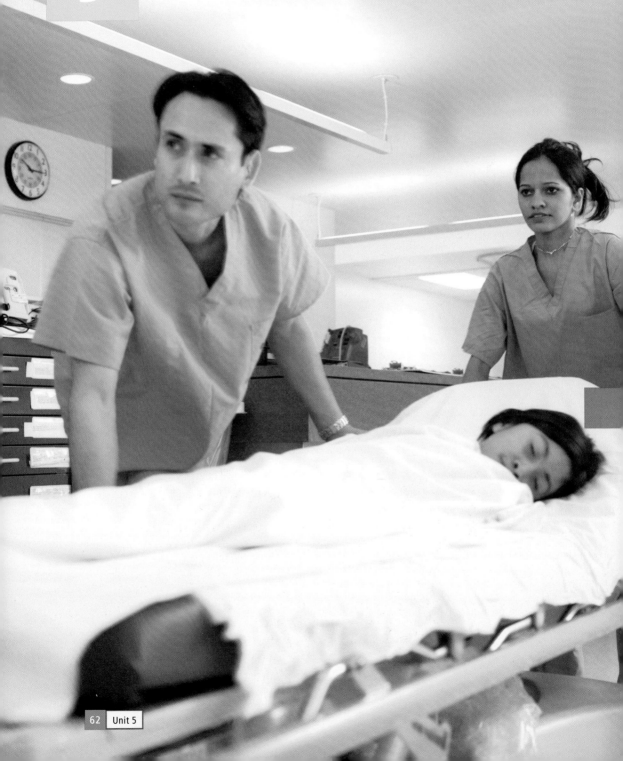

UNIT

5

Communication and Teamwork

Identifying and describing strategic use of effective communication skills

Recognizing the characteristics of a good team member

Identifying the elements of a successful team

ollywood shows it as dramatic chaos: A gurney carrying a critically injured patient crashes through swinging doors! The scene is filled with shouting emergency room personnel. In real life, however, a working trauma team is actually calm and quiet. Each member of the trauma team has a very specific role, and every member knows how his or her tasks support what other team members must do. Everyone on the team shares the goal of saving the patient. They must work quickly and accurately under high pressure. If a trauma team member doesn't understand or perform her role—or if he is unsure of another member's actions—the patient may die. Of course, not every team addresses life-and-death situations. Nor is every team made up of members with such clearly defined roles. But all types of teams are composed of people working together for a common purpose. Effective teamwork depends on several important factors; among them are understanding the purposes and goals of the team, using effective communication, and combining and building on team member strengths.

Understanding the Power of Communication

Before you can apply good communication to teamwork, you need to know the keys to effective communication. A good communicator possesses good speaking skills and good listening skills. Think about a team you've been a part of, such as a school project or even the planning of a family event. Which person on the team would you consider the best communicator? Chances are it was a person who communicated clearly and listened to what you had to say. Skilled communicators are people who speak well *and* listen well.

Listening to Understand Others

It is common to hear what a person says without fully understanding what the person's words mean. To be a good listener, you have to apply **active listening,** which involves paying attention to the speaker, making a conscious effort not only to hear but also to comprehend others in conversation. Active listening is especially important on teams, because there are more voices, more ideas, and more opinions. In order to be a good listener, you must take responsibility for comprehending, or understanding, the message that a speaker is sending. The following steps describe active listening skills behaviors.

Give the speaker your full attention. Teams must often gather in places with distractions and interruptions all around. However, giving the speaker your full attention is the most important behavior in active listening.

Pay attention to *how* words are said. The tone of words can change their meaning, even if they are the exact same words. Sometimes tone can be obvious—the difference between kindness and sarcasm is clear. But tone can also be subtle. As a listener, if you disregard your speaker's tone of voice, you miss part of the message, which can lead to misunderstandings and create problems on a team.

Look at the speaker as directly as possible. There is no single way to interpret body movement during conversation. For example, standing with arms crossed can show anger or discomfort; shrugging shoulders can show uncertainty or irritation. But facial expressions and body language can help you understand a speaker's meaning.

To improve your listening skills so that you can work well on a team, you can form an active listening strategy. A strategy is a careful and deliberate plan or method. Developing an active listening strategy requires commitment and practice. You won't always be able to eliminate all distractions and interruptions during your discussions. But doing the following will help you be a better communicator:

Face the person to whom you are talking directly. Maintain eye contact and be aware of your own body language. Keep in mind that you send nonverbal messages that affect the conversation.

Don't interrupt. This can be difficult, especially on a team where everyone wants to share an idea or clarify someone else's idea. Letting the other person finish speaking before you respond shows respect for others on your team.

Restate what you hear. The speaker will then know if he or she needs to clarify, or explain the point in different words. Don't pretend you understand another person's message. Instead, ask questions for clarification.

Practice
Critical Thinking

Consider the two listeners below. What active listening strategies can Marcus and Sara use to improve communication and teamwork?

- Marcus used to work in IT before he became a medical technician. When he calls the hospital's IT department, he often interrupts the help desk specialist because he feels he knows how to fix what is wrong. Marcus doesn't understand why the help desk specialist's tone is sometimes impatient and angry.

- Sara doesn't like to talk in staff meetings at the doctor's office, where she works as a medical billing and coding specialist. She rarely makes eye contact, staring at her cell phone instead. When the meetings are over, she almost always has questions but doesn't ask them. She knows that if she's doing something wrong, her boss will email her.

As a member of a team, what would be your active listening strategy? You might encourage your group to have their conversation away from distractions. You can make a point of turning off your cell phone and invite others to do the same. Encourage your group to sit around a table or in a circle, facing each other. Look directly at each person as he or she speaks. Listen to each person without interrupting. When you have the opportunity to respond throughout the discussion, address each person in the group at one point or another. Ask each person at least one question and confirm that you understand everyone's points.

Speaking to Share Ideas and Persuade Others

You know that active listening is important, but somebody has to do the talking. Carrying on a casual conversation with friends comes naturally. But in team settings, it is important to constantly work at speaking more effectively.

In the workplace, most conversations revolve around the need to get things done. When you have a job, you belong to a group of people who share a purpose. You are part of a team assembled to meet certain goals. You read about long- and short-term goals in Unit 2. Goals are objectives that you can achieve through your actions. **Problem solving** is the mental process for moving from a present situation toward a goal. Work teams cooperate to reach goals, practicing continuous problem solving.

Problem solving is a step-by-step process. It is rare for one person to complete the steps alone. Other team members are usually involved, and the team members must communicate. Communication involves both speaking and listening. As with listening, effective speaking can require a strategy.

When you speak, you typically have a purpose for doing so. But how aware are you of that purpose when you talk? Knowing your own purpose is the foundation of an effective speaking strategy. Before you open your mouth to speak, ask yourself, "What is it that I want to achieve?"

- Do I want to share information with others?
- Do I need to get information from others?
- Do I want to express support for ideas?
- Do I want to persuade others to see things differently?

Effective speakers know what they want. And they get to the point and support their position with convincing evidence. However, abruptly stating what you want as a demand may not be an effective speaking strategy. Persuasion is more effective. **Persuasion** is the act of influencing a person's values, beliefs, attitudes, or behaviors. An effective speaker is persuasive without being offensive or demanding. A persuasive speaker also knows that his or her style affects the mood and reactions of others.

You can help control the messages you convey by managing your verbal and nonverbal behaviors. At school, you may be asked to work on teams to complete projects or study new information. It's important to communicate effectively so you can get the most out of the team and offer your best to team members.

Control the speed at which you speak. Speaking too slowly can make you sound monotonous or insecure, and speaking too quickly can make you sound nervous.

Control the volume at which you speak. Speaking too loudly can sound aggressive. Speaking too softly makes it more difficult for people to hear you. Make sure your volume matches your surroundings. You wouldn't speak loudly in a hospital, for example, and you wouldn't whisper at a football game.

Speak clearly. Mumbling conveys a lack of confidence and suggests that you attach little importance to what you have to say. Consciously enunciating, or saying each word clearly, helps you emphasize key points.

Make eye contact. Observe how your listeners are reacting as you speak.

Know what you want to say before opening your mouth. Do not be afraid of pausing to collect your thoughts. Then be brief. In teams it is important to get to your point and then stop speaking so you can listen to others' ideas or opinions.

Be considerate. Be sensitive to others who may wish to speak, and invite them to reply.

You can improve your speaking strategies just as you improve your listening strategies—with practice. Choose one characteristic of your speaking style that you want to strengthen to make yourself more persuasive. For example, if you tend to get loud when you are excited, pay special attention to controlling your volume until a more moderate tone becomes habit. If people regularly ask you to repeat yourself, assess whether you are speaking too quickly or quietly. Work on refining one characteristic of your speaking style at a time.

A good speaker on a team practices all the skills of effective persuasion between individuals, plus more. In team communication, individual members can present many points of view on an issue. Naturally, each individual wants others to share his or her perspective, or point of view. Some team members might be patient about differing opinions; others might take offense from differing opinions, or worse yet, behave offensively toward those who offer them. When people disagree about what is important or about the best way to solve a problem, it can produce tension, or even conflict.

Research has shown that "person-oriented" conflict (such as disagreements over personal views about politics and religion) hinders effective team performance, while "task-related" conflict (such as disagreements over which tasks should be performed and how) promotes effective team performance.[1] A good team communicator does not shy away from disagreement, but instead practices active conflict resolution. **Conflict resolution** is the process of arriving at solutions while taking the interests of all parties into account. It involves listening, evaluating, prioritizing, and compromising. The more people involved in a conflict, the more complicated it is to resolve. Though the process of conflict resolution involves listening to everyone's needs and interests,

[1] Garcia-Prieto, P., Bellard, E., & Schneider, S.C. (2003). Experiencing diversity, conflict, and emotions in teams. *Applied Psychology: An International Review*, 52(3), 413–440. doi:10.1111/1464-0597.00142

it is close to impossible to find a solution that makes everyone happy. So, the goal of conflict resolution has to be consensus. **Consensus** is a decision agreed upon by *most* of the people concerned.

How can a skilled team speaker facilitate conflict resolution? A skilled speaker can help by clearly restating the different sides of an argument so that other team members can compare all the points of view. And to avoid worsening the conflict, the team speaker can present each side by using proven speaking strategies: speaking slowly, speaking in a low voice, enunciating, using eye contact, being brief, and being considerate. Of course, the speaker has his or her opinion about which side is the "right" side. But after clarifying the positions in an argument, a strong team speaker's job is to try to persuade others to compromise. Persuasion is a powerful skill in building consensus.

True Story

"In my company, the sales team and product delivery team were always at each other's throats. The product people complained that the sales people would promise a customer anything to get a sale, even if it was something impossible. The sales people complained that the product people didn't care what customers really wanted. To solve the problem, our company president made a weekly cross-team meeting, where the sales people talk about potential sales, and the product people talk about what's possible. There's still plenty of conflict, but there's also respect. Now, we surface the problems early, when we still have time to change the contract."

Applying Individual Strengths to a Team

In our personal lives, we have the freedom to choose our friends—we can spend more time with people we like and limit or eliminate contact with people we dislike. However, we do not have this freedom at work. Team members come and go, and you are almost guaranteed to dislike some of your co-workers. You may even have overt conflict with someone upon whom you depend in order to do your job. This is why teamwork skills are so important. You must find a way to work well with everyone, even the people you would rather avoid.

Identifying Team Member Strengths

We routinely work in groups in our daily lives. A family in a household shares chores; a small group of students cooperates on a project; a department in the workplace functions as a team. Some teams are assembled deliberately. Members are selected for their specific skills. Other teams are formed without consideration of the skills that members bring, and members' strengths must be identified after the fact.

Teams are made up of individuals, and individual people are unique. Skills that distinguish you—things you consistently do especially well—are your strengths. By now you should know what your strengths are, as well as your weaknesses—the skills you need to improve. Everyone has strengths and weaknesses—we can't be good at *everything*. Figure 5.1 shows a few strengths and weaknesses that people might possess and that are especially relevant to teamwork:

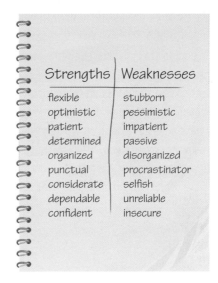

Strengths	Weaknesses
flexible	stubborn
optimistic	pessimistic
patient	impatient
determined	passive
organized	disorganized
punctual	procrastinator
considerate	selfish
dependable	unreliable
confident	insecure

Figure 5.1

Your strengths and weaknesses determine how you go about tasks and how hard you need to work at those tasks. Suppose, for example, you discover that a new window installed in your house leaks. You need to arrange to have it replaced under warranty. If you are not a confident speaker but you write well, you may choose to write a letter to the company to request the replacement. If you communicate better orally than in writing, you would probably choose to make a phone call or visit the store instead. However, if impatience is one of your weaknesses, the letter still might be the more effective approach for you!

When a team approaches a goal, it makes sense to match the talents of team members to the tasks for which they are best suited. This requires all team members to know their own strengths and share those strengths with the team. Communication style is just one way of many in which individuals differ. If you have a team member who is known to be systematic and organized, he or she might be the best person to break down tasks and suggest how they should be distributed to team members. But if you have a known procrastinator on a team, you probably do not want that person to be in charge of making sure everyone is completing tasks on time.

In addition to individual strengths that members bring to a team effort, people also possess certain strengths that make them better team members in general. These are the traits that make a person a good co-worker. Which of the following apply to you?

- Dependable
- Honest
- Trusting of other team members
- Open to new ideas
- Enthusiastic
- Effective communicator
- Willing to share credit
- Encouraging
- Supportive

Motivating Team Members

Just because people know what their strengths are does not mean they automatically feel comfortable sharing them with others. Nor does it mean they are immediately willing to apply those strengths on a team. Knowing how they fit in with a team can help with their motivation. **Motivation** is something that provides incentive to act, or encouragement to do something.

It takes time for team members to get to know and trust each other. You probably participated in icebreaker or team-building exercises when you first found yourself in a situation with new people. Maybe you played a simple communication game like "telephone" or a cooperation game in which you had to instruct a blindfolded partner to perform a basic task. These activities are usually fun, but they can seem like a waste of time because they are unrelated to your team's goals.

The point of team-building exercises is to introduce team members to one another in a low-stress environment that is fun but still requires people to work together to achieve a common objective. Although they may seem a little embarrassing at first, team-building exercises can be very effective at creating team spirit. They encourage team members to communicate and help members discover one another's personalities. Team-building exercises are not only useful when members meet each other for the first time, they can also help existing teams practice consensus building and problem solving. In all cases, team-building exercises require participants to observe and listen to their peers. Here are a few examples:

Ice Breaking: Two Truths and a Lie. Participants have a few moments to list three things about themselves on a piece of paper. Pairs trade papers and use them to introduce their partners to the whole group. The group tries to decide which two details are true and which one is untrue.

Consensus Building: Shipwrecked. Small teams must determine which five items they would choose to have with them if they knew there was a chance they might be stranded on an island. Each team presents and defends its list to the larger group.

Problem Solving: Bridge the Gap. Teams use drinking straws and paperclips (no tape or glue allowed) to build a bridge between two surfaces that are farther apart than the length of the straws. Teams compete by progressively adding weight (coins, for example) to their completed bridges to see whose holds the greatest load.

Activities such as these are fun, and they build camaraderie. Most importantly, though, they reveal characteristics of individuals and how people work with others. Playing Two Truths and a Lie can reveal who in a group is the most creative or convincing. Group interaction during Shipwrecked can reveal who is good at facilitating a consensus. Bridge the Gap can reveal the planners and the risk takers.

Informal team games also reveal the dominant leaders in the group. In a formal work situation, the role of leader is given by authority to the person in the managerial position, whether or not that person possesses natural leadership skills. But in less formal, leaderless groups, a leader almost always emerges based on personality. Some people have a tendency to take charge, while others do not. Scandinavian researchers have identified five different leadership styles: rational, intuitive, dependent, avoidant, and spontaneous.[2] In a study of leadership, they determined that elected leaders (as opposed to appointed leaders) tend to be more spontaneous and intuitive and less rational, dependent, or avoidant. People who are spontaneous and intuitive are perceived as forceful and decisive, which are qualities that others will respect and follow.[3] However, teams need to be cautious about following the dominant leader and not listening to the quieter members of the team. Research has shown that less dominant members of the team often hold the best solutions to the team's problems and can set the tone for the entire team.[4] Effective teams determine and utilize the strengths of all team members, not just the natural leaders.

True Story

"I'm a medical assistant in a specialist's practice. My job is clinical, so I deal with patients. Other types of assistants do the clerical and administrative tasks. The office admin manager wanted to hold some big brainstorming meeting about giving patients a better experience. I didn't see why I had to participate. I do my job. The scheduling, reception, record keeping, filing, and billing are other people's jobs that don't concern me. I don't need them telling me what to do. I didn't see how getting the whole office team together could make a difference. Well, was I wrong! We talked about every step it takes our office team to serve a patient from start to finish. It turns out that all of our jobs are connected—each person's job affects another person's job. By learning what we were doing 'the hard way,' we were able to change a few of our processes and shorten our average patient's waiting time by ten minutes."

[2] Scott, S.G. & Bruce, R.A. (1995). Decision-making style: The development and assessment of a new measure. *Educational and Psychological Measurement, 55*(5), 818–831.

[3] Thunholm, P. (2009). Military leaders and followers—do they have different decision styles? *Scandinavian Journal of Psychology, 50*(4), 317–324. doi:10.1111/j.1467-9450.2009.00714.x

[4] Weis, M.J. (2005). Quiet leadership. *Leader to Leader, 2005,* 39–47. Retrieved from EBSCOhost.

What Is the Purpose of a Team?

You've read a lot in this unit about people interacting in different settings. And you've read that active communication and identifying strengths can help people interact in groups. Not every group is a *team*, though. What do you think of first when you see the word *team*? A sports team with a coach who's in charge and players who each have a specific position? Or maybe that trauma team rushing to save a life in the ER? Both are good examples, and they satisfy the basic definition of *team*—a group of individuals working together to accomplish a common objective. It is the common purpose that makes a group a team. A team itself and every person on it has a **function,** which is the purpose for which something is designed or the action for which a person's role is identified.

Characteristics of a Team

Teamwork makes it possible to reach goals that a single person could achieve alone only with difficulty, if at all. Suppose you have to move 100 cartons of files into storage. Working alone, even loading several cartons at a time onto a cart, you would make many trips to get the job done. If three others shared the work with you, it would get done in a quarter of the time. Now consider that the files are not simply being moved from one room to another. The cartons must be sorted and distributed to different departments. Perhaps, instead of all four of you hauling files, you sort and label the cartons with their destinations, another person loads the cartons while grouping them by department, and two others make the deliveries. All four team members are contributing to the accomplishment of the goal, yet you fill different roles and perform different tasks.

How would you decide who would sort and label, who would load, and who would distribute the files? The sensible way, of course, would be to match team member strengths with tasks. You might have the most knowledge about which files go to which departments. The person loading the batches knows less about that,

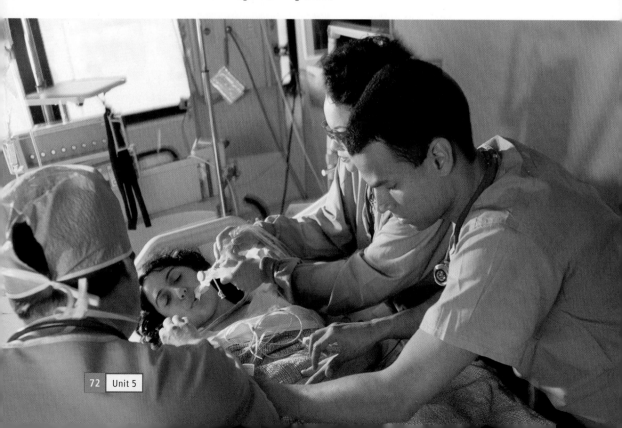

but is strong and organized. The two making deliveries don't know anything about the files, but they know their way around the facility and can get the deliveries made quickly. The team is more powerful than the individuals alone because it combines all of their knowledge and capabilities, improving problem-solving.

Every team has member roles, whether or not they are clearly defined and assigned to specific people. On a sports team, the roles are clearly defined; in many school and work teams, they are not. On some teams, the same team member fills the same role, and completes the same tasks, all the time. In other situations, team members may trade roles, sharing responsibilities and completing different tasks at different times in a process known as cross-training.

Often, in the workplace, more attention is paid to individual roles than to the team as a whole. For example, think about a company in which all of the employees have written job descriptions. Each individual does only the tasks on his or her job description. If everybody does their jobs, all the employees get the support they need from other team members, and the company reaches its goals. Even though the emphasis is on individuals filling their roles, they are still part of a team.

Whether or not they are managed through a formal process, certain roles emerge consistently in team situations. Somebody usually takes the lead in breaking the team goal into individual tasks, assigning those tasks to individuals, and keeping track of progress. On a formal work team, this is the role of the manager. On a less formal team, such as a study group, members volunteer for the project tasks they prefer. Team members will then have to negotiate who will handle tasks that nobody wants.

Teams need a way for members to figure out the tasks that must be done to meet the goal.

And members need a way to find out what their roles and tasks are. In a formal team, a strong designated leader might determine all assignments and delegate the tasks with no negotiation. In less formal collaborations, team members meet to discuss the work at hand and the best ways to get it done. Like teams themselves, team meetings can be formal and structured or casual and relaxed. They can also be chaotic, unfocused, and ineffective. You have, no doubt, experienced meetings that dragged on and on, where nobody got anything done.

For a team meeting to be effective, it must have a specific purpose. For example, the purpose might be to determine the strengths of members or to identify sources of materials. During an effective team meeting, all participants must use the best communication practices that you read about in the first section of this unit. Poor communication in a team meeting almost always leads to poor performance. Active listening and persuasive speaking help build consensus, avoid conflict, and resolve conflict when it occurs. In good team meetings, members stay focused on the task and conclude their discussions within a reasonably brief time.

Park Clean-up Team Meeting

April 24th, 7:00 to 8:00 p.m.

Agenda items:
- **Introduction of new members**
- **Progress on last week's assignments**
- **Report on donations**
- **List of supplies we still need**
- **Assignments: action items for next week**
- **Any other concerns?**
- **Schedule next meeting**

Figure 5.2 Sample meeting agenda

In a meeting, team members take on additional roles, such as planner, organizer, resource gatherer, delegator, facilitator, interpreter, peacekeeper, time manager, and/or general problem solver. How often a team should meet depends on too many factors for there to be one right answer. But generally, every team member should leave each meeting with a task, or an action item, to complete before the next meeting. When the next meeting occurs, it should begin with a summary of the tasks completed by the members between meetings.

Building **Background**

Students often write papers and complete homework assignments on their own. Individual homework is often easier to complete than group projects. But individual homework is an artificial situation; rarely in "real life" will you be asked to take an assignment home, produce a result alone, and not collaborate with anyone else. In the workplace, nearly all assignments require teamwork, even if you have limited interaction with your teammates. When you do a team assignment for school, you learn new content, but you also practice teamwork skills that are very important outside the academic environment.

The Life of a Team

A team exists for a purpose: to achieve a goal. What happens when the goal is met? Of course, some goals are ongoing. A retailer with a goal of selling computers will maintain a team to keep selling computers as long as it is successful. A team also can be formed to solve a temporary problem, and once that problem is solved, there is no need for the team to remain together. A parent team formed to raise funds to replace a school's playground equipment could dissolve once it has raised enough money.

How can you tell if a team has served its purpose or continues to serve it? How can you tell if the team is functioning well? A team's performance must be evaluated. Your performance at work is evaluated, and your work at school is graded. In both cases, you learn how you have met expectations and ways you can improve. Evaluation measures your success and guides what you do next. The same is true for the evaluation of a team. The fundraising parent team mentioned earlier would be evaluated as successful if it raised enough money to buy new playground equipment. What about the computer sales team? The sales team might be evaluated as successful if it sold enough computers to reach its sales goal. However, if the sales team did not meet its sales goal because a few of its sales members did not communicate well with their customers, the team would be evaluated as unsuccessful.

Teams have "life cycles." They function differently during different stages. There is not a concrete set of steps that every team goes through in exact order, and many of the stages overlap. Here are some general team stages:

Identification of the goal or problem. A reason appears for the team to exist.

Team formation. Team members are identified and assigned or recruited. The team goal is broken into tasks, tasks are associated with roles, and roles are assigned to members.

Launch and motivation. Members comprehend what they are to do, how to go about it, and why it matters. Work begins.

Routine operation. All members continue completing tasks. The team meets as needed, marking progress, measuring success, and making ongoing adjustments. Effective teamwork makes or breaks the success of the team.

Milestone evaluation. *Milestone* is a figurative term for a significant event. A team performs ongoing evaluation to measure completion of smaller tasks. More thorough evaluation should occur at important times, such as annually or at the end of a project.

Conclusion or evolution. If a team has achieved its goal or solved its problem, it can cease to exist. Or, it might take on a new goal. A team with continuous goals carries on. The continuous team will likely change over time, though. It will evolve as the goals do. It will function differently as members change and their roles evolve.

In many cases, teams can achieve far greater success than individuals. However, teams don't always succeed. Teamwork can be complicated. Diverse personalities of individuals with different priorities can make it very difficult to get all team members "on the same page." If a team lacks members with necessary strengths, or if members' talents are poorly matched with their roles, motivation can weaken. If team members have poor communication habits, confusion and conflict can set in. How can a team overcome such flaws and avoid failure? The answer almost always has to do with communication. As you learned in the first section of this unit, communication is very powerful, and listening comes before speaking for a reason.

If things on a team aren't going well, somebody has to say so. On a formal, structured team, it is the leader's role to manage the team's performance and provide coaching when there is a need for improvement. In a less formal

May 10th Park Clean-up
Team Evaluation

Role	Team Members	Performance: 1–5 (1 = could have done better; 5 = fantastic!)	Comments
Volunteer recruitment			
Materials donations			
Refreshments			
Worker registration			
Child care			
Thank-you notes			
Publicity			

Figure 5.3 Sample team evaluation form

team without a designated leader, team members must evaluate themselves and each other. That is not always easy. Team members who note problems and want to bring about change must offer only constructive criticism. **Constructive criticism** is a well-meant evaluation, intended to help a person improve some aspect of his or her performance. Constructive criticism never involves accusation or blame. A good strategy for offering constructive criticism is to offer it as a request, not a complaint, and try to pair it with a positive observation. For example, instead of saying to a school teammate, "You're not doing your fair share," try, "You've made some good observations, and our project would be better with more from you. Where else can we get you involved?"

But even the most well-meant observation can leave others feeling defensive and unfairly singled out. That is why it is essential to listen carefully and speak with sensitivity on a team. If you are on the receiving end of constructive criticism, listen actively for the good intentions behind the message. If you are on the delivering end of such a message, share your ideas persuasively about how the whole team might better reach its goals. These strategies will help you and your team be more successful.

Unit Summary

- Active listening and persuasive speaking are communication strategies that can help people interact well in groups.
- People have different strengths. Matching individuals' strengths to their roles on a team will ensure better performance from team members and from the team as a whole.
- Team members who know the other team members and where they fit in will be more motivated.
- Different types of teams still have similar roles for members to fill.
- Teams change over time, and some cease to exist. Teams must evaluate their performance through their life cycles and continually adjust.

TO-DO List

- ✔ Be an active listener in every conversation.
- ✔ Make a list of ways your strengths are matched to the tasks you perform in team roles.
- ✔ Find ways to improve the alignment of your talents to your team tasks.
- ✔ Join a community service group that functions as a team with a goal of improving some aspect of the area where you live.

Important Terms

How well do you know these terms? Look them up in the glossary if you need help remembering them.

active listening

problem solving

persuasion

conflict resolution

consensus

motivation

function

constructive criticism

Exercises

1. Observe the people with whom you regularly interact. Look for examples of active listening and persuasive speaking. Write a few sentences to describe your observations of each behavior. If you do not observe anyone applying active listening or persuasive speaking, describe a situation in which each would have been useful, perhaps to build consensus or avoid or resolve a conflict.

2. Write two to three paragraphs describing a successful team that you admire. The team you choose could be formal, such as a business or a sports team, or it could be a more informal group, such as a parents' group or a community service group. No matter what team you choose, make sure the team is made up of many individuals working toward a common goal. In your paper, identify the various strengths of the individual team members and write about how each team member contributes to the success of the team.

3. Suppose you are part of a team on which one member routinely criticizes the performance of others in a negative way. How would you present constructive criticism to try to change the situation? Write a script of the conversation you would have, including what you anticipate others would say.

Identifying reading strategies to improve comprehension

Utilizing relevant pre- and post-reading strategies

Using reading strategies for academic purposes

Employing strategies for meaningful online reading

don't worry, you're not alone. Most students find it tough to get excited about reading textbooks. They just aren't as much fun to read as magazines or mystery novels, not to mention your Facebook page or Twitter feed! The material can be hard to understand and even harder to remember. What better sleep aid could there be than a nice, thick textbook, right?

But you need to know the material in those textbooks. It's important, not only to get a good grade in the class, but also so you can recall important knowledge on the job after you graduate. Depending on what you will do for a living, remembering what was in that textbook could be a matter of life and death. Developing good reading habits can make a big difference to your success, both in school and in life. Even if you are an excellent student, you can improve your reading skills and your comprehension and retention of difficult texts. It just takes some strategy. If you learn the handful of incredibly useful reading strategies in this unit, you will be much more effective in navigating textbooks, both print and online.

Strategies for Pre-reading

The prefix *pre-* means before or in advance, so **pre-reading** strategies are those you use *before reading*. How can you use reading strategies *before* you even read anything? Simple—using strategies that prepare your brain not only helps you understand what you read, but it helps you remember it, too.

Consider How Your Memory Works

In order to be an effective reader, you need to remember what you have just read so that you can use the information later. Scientists who study memory and learning have proven that we are more likely to remember a new idea if we already know something about the subject. For example, if I say "sesquipedalian" to you right now and then walk out of the room, what is the probability that you are going to remember that word in five minutes, in one hour, a week from now? Chances are high that you have never heard that word before (that is, it doesn't relate to anything you already know something about), so you will forget it pretty much immediately. Now, what if I say "digicam"? You might not really know what a digicam is, but you probably have some experience with this word. *Digi* sounds like *digital*, so it's likely to be something electronic; *cam* sounds like *camera*, so it may have a lens or a visual element. In fact, you'd probably guess that it's some kind of digital camera, and you'd be right. Because you have previous experience with related words, the probability that you will remember this new word a week from now is much higher. An image will come to mind that you can use for recall. The information you already know (such as the meanings of *digital* and *camera*) can be used as **scaffolding,** a supporting framework upon which you can build, attaching the new information. (In case

you're dying to know by now, *sesquipedalian* means "of or related to long words or many syllables," so a sesquipedalian news anchor would be a news anchor who used a lot of long words.)

So, you need to know something about the subject in order to remember it, but that seems like a paradox, doesn't it? Aren't you doing the reading exactly so that you can learn about something *new*, something that you don't know anything about yet? How on earth are you going to remember it, then? Well, the good news is that there are some simple strategies for tricking your brain into rapidly creating new scaffolding so that you can remember the brand new information in your textbook. These strategies fall in the category of pre-reading, a series of brief activities that you can complete before you begin your focused reading.

View the Pictures

The first strategy for creating scaffolding is to quickly review all of the photos and diagrams in the unit (if there are any). Images are appealing and easy to remember, so starting with the images will create an important foundation for your scaffolding. Look at the images and read the captions—they will give you an overview of the reading.

Identify Your Purpose for Reading

The next scaffolding strategy is to decide why you're going to read this new information. Your brain is much more likely to engage in and remember something it thinks is important. So, you need to convince yourself that this reading is important! Before you start reading, ask yourself, "Why has my instructor assigned this reading? What does she want me to get out of it?" Your brain is much more likely to pick out and remember critical information if you have told it what matters in advance. To do this, go to each section heading and turn it into a question in your mind. For instance, in the example that follows, the heading on the page is *Liability Issues Faced by Loss Prevention Specialists*. Ask yourself, "What are some liability issues faced by loss prevention specialists?" Now you have a purpose for reading—you need to find out what those liability issues are. Then ask yourself why you need to know this information. How will it be helpful in your future career? By identifying a purpose for reading, you will engage your brain, and you will be able to identify critical information and filter details that do not suit your purpose.

Answer the Questions

If there are questions at the end of the unit, you can use one of the best pre-reading techniques of all—making up answers to the questions. WHAT? That's right, you haven't read the unit yet, but just make up answers to the questions at the end. Your brain is naturally curious, so if you pose a question, it will want to know the answer. It will even have a tendency to guess, or make up its own answer. So, help it along. You are much more likely to remember things that are repetitive, unusual, absurd, ridiculous, colorful, large, dramatic, scary, disgusting, or full of motion. So, when you make up your answers, make them creative! For example, let's say that the question at the end of the unit said, "What does sesquipedalian mean?" If you didn't already know, you might think something like this: "Well, *sesqui* sounds like *Sasquatch*, which is the Yeti or Abominable Snowman, and *pedal* means "foot," like a bike pedal, so *sesquipedalian* must be a gigantic Yeti pedaling down the Alps on a massive yellow bike!" Your made-up answer could be entirely different from this, but you get the idea—use humor, colors, motion, size, and anything imaginative as you make up the answer. Then, when you

read the unit later and find out that *sesquipedalian* means "wordy," imagine your surprise! You will be much more interested (and much more likely to remember the whole experience) than if you hadn't tried to answer the questions at the end of the unit.

Read the Boldface Terms

If there are vocabulary words or terms in boldface in the unit, you can build your scaffolding by reading each term and the sentence around it. Learning key terms before you read will help you read more efficiently.

Write down the boldface terms on a piece of paper as you read them. After you have read the unit, you can decide which ones are important enough for you to copy the word and its definition into your notes or onto flashcards.

Skim the Text

The last pre-reading strategy is to skim the text. During **skimming,** you quickly run your eyes across the whole text, line by line, just to get a sense of the organization of the text and the way the subject is explained. Skimming gives you a heads-up before you start your focused reading. Try it. Skim the sample page from the loss prevention manual on the next page. Take ten seconds to gloss over the boldface titles and subheadings to get an idea of the organization. What is this unit about? What will you learn

from it? Research has shown that our brains can process a great deal of information in just a "blink." Take a few seconds to skim the text.

Building **Background**

Text features to look out for when you read:

- Heading, subheading: signal of a new topic

- Photo, illustration, diagram, chart: embellishment or explanation of information in the text

- Highlighted, boldface, or italicized word: key vocabulary, title

- Caption: explanation of photo, illustration, diagram, or chart

- Side column call-outs: piece of featured information that is related to the main text

- Label for image: detail or information about the image

Chapter 5

Liability Issues Faced by Loss Prevention Specialists

The job of a loss prevention specialist is to protect the company's assets. When an employee of the company is accused of wrongdoing, the specialist may need to interrogate that employee. The specialist should be aware of liability issues that may arise from his or her interrogation techniques. Should the accused employee decide to file a lawsuit, the resulting monetary damages could far outweigh the cost of the original investigation. Here are some situations that may lead to a lawsuit:

One-on-one interviews can safeguard against false imprisonment claims.

False Imprisonment A person need not be physically restrained to claim false imprisonment. False imprisonment is defined as "intentional detention of a person by another person who is not lawfully authorized to do so." Here are factors that courts consider in a false imprisonment claim:

- Freedom of movement of accused person
- Interrogator blocking an exit door
- Interrogators outnumbering, or "ganging up" on, accused person
- Unreasonably lengthy interrogation sessions with no breaks
- Interrogation taking place behind locked doors
- Seating arrangement during interrogation

To protect against a false imprisonment claim, a specialist may instill a sense of privacy by conducting the interview one on one. However, a third party may be needed as a witness, such as when there exists probable threat of an employee making unwarranted misconduct accusations against an interrogator. In such cases, the witness should stand quietly behind the employee's chair as the main interrogator conducts the interview.

Aggressive Interrogations A confession obtained through coercion may be considered improperly obtained evidence. Coercion refers to the use of physical force, whether real or perceived. The statement "You're not going home until you confess" constitutes coercion. If this improperly obtained confession is used as evidence to terminate the employee, the employee may file a wrongful discharge suit.

Figure 6.1 Sample manual page

Strategies During Reading

After viewing the pictures, turning the headings into questions, making up answers to the questions at the end of the unit, reviewing the boldface terms, and skimming the unit, you may feel as if you have already done your reading! However, after you have done your pre-reading a few times, building your scaffolding will become a habit that takes no more than a few minutes. With your scaffolding built, you are ready for focused reading. As you read, keep on being strategic. Here are some strategies to use *while you're reading* that will help you both to understand and to remember.

Ask Questions

Remember how effective it was to make up answers to the questions at the end of the unit? Even if there are no questions, you can make up your own. Keep playing to your inquisitive nature. As you read, you will probably find yourself asking questions about the text. When questions come to mind, write them down—you can use self-stick, paper, or electronic notes. You may run across the answers later in the text. Or, you may want to bring the questions to class and ask a classmate or your instructor. Typical questions might include:

- Why is _____ important?
- What just happened? What will happen next?
- What caused _____?
- Why don't I understand this paragraph/section?

What good questions can I ask as I read this lesson?

Create a K-W-L Chart

If you know that what you are reading is very important, and you find the material very difficult or dense (full of definitions, lots of details, or many words you do not understand), then a great strategy is to create a K-W-L chart. This handy tool is known as a before, during, and after organizer because it allows you to record what you **K**now about the topic *before* reading, **W**hat you want to learn *during* reading, and what you have **L**earned *after* you finished reading. Figure 6.2 below provides an example.

Before you start reading, write in the **K** column what you already know. This is a good place to put the vocabulary terms you learned during pre-reading, anything you learned from viewing the pictures, and any key comments your instructor made in class. Then, in the **W** column, write what you want to know. This is where you should put your unit headings that you turned into questions during pre-reading. Then keep

K – What I Know	W – What I Want to Know	L – What I Learned
Loss prevention specialists protect a company's assets. Loss prevention specialists catch shoplifters and other wrongdoers.	What are some liability issues that loss prevention specialists face? How can a loss prevention specialist protect the company from a lawsuit?	

Figure 6.2 K-W-L Chart

your chart next to you as you read. As you read, you will find answers to the things you want to know. Enter them in the **L** column as the concepts you learn while you are reading. The K-W-L chart is a terrific tool for medical texts, complex trades texts with schematics and formulas, legal texts, and any other difficult reading material.

Find the Main Idea

Another strategy that aids in reading comprehension is finding the **main idea.** The main idea of a paragraph is the most important piece of information the author wants to convey about the topic of the paragraph. The details of the paragraph support the main idea by telling who, what, when, where, or why. The details explain or prove the main idea. Sometimes the main idea is explicitly expressed, often at the beginning of a paragraph. Other times the main idea is merely implied, and you need to find it and state it in your own words. Read each paragraph of the passage below, from the oral hygiene unit of a dental assisting manual. Then, from the two choices provided, choose the main idea of each paragraph.

Do you know the main idea?

Paragraph 1: The main idea can often be found in the opening sentence of the paragraph. In this case, the first sentence (answer choice *a*) states the main idea explicitly. Notice that the rest of the sentences in the paragraph are details that support the main idea—they list various ways to position yourself relative to the patient. In other words, they answer the question, "What are some ways to position yourself relative to the patient?" Answer choice *b* is clearly not the main idea; in fact, it seems to contradict it. According to the passage, it *does* make a difference whether you sit or stand relative to the patient.

Paragraph 2: The main idea of this paragraph is actually repeated three different ways: 1) use simple language in your oral hygiene instructions; 2) avoid scientific terms; 3) educate and encourage the patient in a professional yet down-to-earth manner. When stating the main idea, you can go with one of the stated ideas, or you can combine the ideas and state the main idea in your own words, as in answer choice *b*. Answer choice *a* is a detail that supports the main idea by giving specific examples of scientific terms versus layman's terms.

---

1. Where you position yourself relative to the patient will influence your ability to create an atmosphere of trust. Stand in front of the patient so that you can make eye contact and establish rapport. When discussing past neglect of oral hygiene, it is preferable to sit on the dental stool so that you are at the same eye level, not looming over the patient and "talking down" to him.

What is the main idea?

a) Your physical positioning will influence the level of trust between you and the patient.

b) It is best to always sit on a dental stool.

2. Use simple language, or layman's terms, in your oral hygiene instructions. Avoid the use of scientific terms unless you know that your patient will understand. Say *above the gum line* instead of *supragingival; tartar* instead of *dental calculus;* and *bad breath* instead of *halitosis.* Your job is to educate and encourage the patient in a professional yet down-to-earth manner.

What is the main idea?

a) Say *above the gum line* instead of *supragingival.*

b) Use simple language, not scientific terms, when instructing and encouraging your patient.

Create a Graphic Organizer

Now that you know how to extract the main idea, you can apply that skill to create a **graphic organizer.** A graphic organizer is a tool that helps you organize your thoughts (and notes). You have already worked with one type of graphic organizer, the K-W-L chart. You can use a graphic organizer for the whole text or a portion of the text that you're trying to figure out. Here are some examples of graphic organizers:

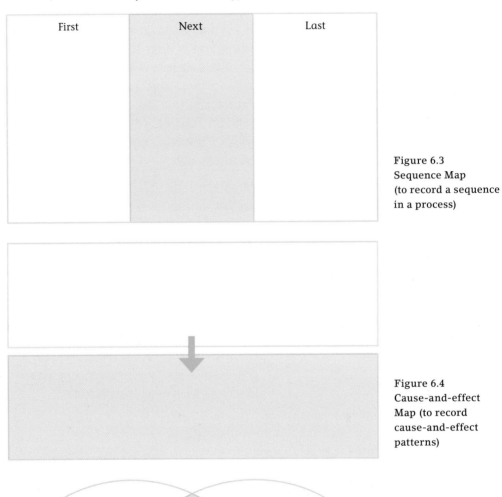

Figure 6.3
Sequence Map
(to record a sequence
in a process)

Figure 6.4
Cause-and-effect
Map (to record
cause-and-effect
patterns)

Figure 6.5
Venn Diagram
(to compare and
contrast information)

Organizational Outline

Another useful graphic organizer is the outline. A standard **outline** form uses Roman and Arabic numerals and upper- and lowercase letters to arrange ideas, details, and examples. Depending on your subject, you may not use all of these levels; however, main ideas should be placed at capital Roman numerals. Secondary ideas are found at uppercase letters and sometimes also Arabic numerals. The details and examples used to support your ideas should be placed at Arabic numerals or lowercase letters, depending on how complex your subject is.

I.
  A.
  B.
    1.
    2.
      a.
      b.
        i.
        ii.

Figure 6.6 Organizational outline
(to form a road map of the reading)

Before you start to make your outline, skim the whole passage to see how it is organized. As you read, identify the main idea of each paragraph. Then go back and read more carefully. You might not use all of the subcategories for every topic. Figure 6.7 is an example of an organizational outline for the loss prevention passage. Try going back to the passage and making your own outline. Then come back and compare it to this one.

Figure 6.7
Sample outline

I. Intro: Loss prevention specialist protects the company's assets; sometimes this involves interrogating someone accused of wrongdoing.

II. Interrogation techniques may expose the company to liability issues.

  A. False imprisonment

    1. Definition: intentional detention by someone who is not lawfully authorized to do so

      a. freedom of movement

      b. blocking exit door

      c. ganging up on accused

      d. long interrogations with no breaks

      e. locked doors

      f. seating arrangement

    2. Protecting against false imprisonment

      a. instill sense of privacy (one-on-one)

      b. third party witness

  B. Aggressive Interrogations

    1. Coercion

      a. definition: use of physical force, real or perceived

      b. confession obtained through coercion

        i. improperly obtained evidence

        ii. may lead to wrongful discharge suit

Summarize

Look at the first line (Item I) in the loss prevention outline. Although the first paragraph in the original passage is very long, for the outline it has been shortened, or summarized, into one brief sentence. Summarizing is one of the most important strategies for students who read a lot and need to retain information. A **summary** is a shorter restatement that contains the most important ideas. When you summarize what you have read, you don't just list the main idea of each paragraph. You synthesize information, which means that you gather bits of information from the entire text to arrive at a few key statements about the text. The following questions and ideas will help you develop a summary:

- What is the main message in the text? What does the author want you to know?
- Which information is/is not important?
- Write a draft of the summary. Is all of the information necessary? What could be omitted?
- Write a text message of the summary to yourself. How precise is it?

TrueStory

"As a secretary in a doctors' office, I perform a wide range of office duties, and I never know what will happen. One day, the office manager hired a transcriptionist to record an important meeting about staff reorganization. The meeting went on and on, and the transcription wound up being 12 pages long. It included every single detail of the session, which was good to have as reference, but this is a busy office—nobody has the time to read all that. I shortened those 12 pages into a 2-page summary. It contained the essential information in an outline form, which was easy to read."

Scan the Text

In some cases, you do not really need to read intensively, but are just searching for specific information. **Scanning,** which is slightly different from skimming, is also a useful strategy during reading. When you scan, you are not reading carefully, word for word. Instead, you are reading with a wide-angle lens to find a specific piece of information very quickly. You already know how to scan. When you look up a word in a dictionary, or when you're trying to find the code for a class during registration, you're scanning. Let's go back to the loss prevention unit again. What is the definition of false imprisonment? You already skimmed the text, so you already came across the definition, but you can't remember the exact wording. Now you need to scan to find the definition for your notes. Lightly make a Z over the page with your finger, and notice the subhead False Imprisonment. This head leads you to the definition, set off in quotation marks: "intentional detention of a person by another person who is not lawfully authorized to do so." Scanning is a useful strategy when you need to find specific information quickly. It is not as useful if you are learning important, new information that you need to be able to reproduce later (for example, on a test).

Strategies for Reading Online Materials

All reading strategies that work for textbooks are effective for online reading. There are also some special strategies for online reading that do not apply to print materials. If you are using a search engine to look for information, much of what you find may not be useful. You will need to scan your results carefully to locate what you need. Online information is not stored or presented in a linear fashion, so you have to think about possible connections between the text you are reading, the text you have just read, and the text you are about to read. Here are a few additional considerations when reading information online:

1. Credibility. Your print textbooks are produced by credible publishers who typically have peer review committees of subject-matter experts review the material. This ensures that statements made in your textbooks are current and accurate. However, the material you read on the Internet has most likely not been through any kind of review process. It is very inexpensive to create a website or blog and publish information. So, much of the information on the Internet is not reliable. Before you use material from a website, you will need to evaluate its credibility:

Blogs, wikis, newsgroups, and listservs. These sources are typically not regulated and not responsible to a branded company, a government, or another authority. Anyone can sign up as a member, and any member can post. As a result, there is no guarantee that the information is anything other than the posting writer's personal opinion. There may be some accurate information, but there may also be falsehoods, and material is likely to show the writer's **bias,** or a personal judgment that is not based on fact.

Commercial (.com) sites. If the website's address ends in .com, it is a commercial site, owned and operated by a company. Some commercial sites are useful for reference information, and commercial sites have the advantage that the company's reputation is at stake if it posts inaccurate information. Information from a commercial site is typically more reliable than that from a blog. However, you must keep in mind that a business is usually trying to sell a product, and the information on its website will show bias toward its interests.

Noncommercial (.edu, .gov, and .org) sites. Noncommercial sites may be educational institutions (.edu), government institutions (.gov), or nonprofit institutions (.org). These sources are typically considered more reliable than commercial sites or blogs because they do not have the profit motive as an incentive to post misleading information. However, each organization has a mission, and its website is likely to show bias toward that mission.

2. Accuracy. Accurate material is typically well organized, clearly written, and correctly spelled. If information is not presented clearly, this is a red flag. A good site will provide sources to support statements of fact. Citations may be an indicator of accuracy, but the best way to determine whether information is accurate is to cross-check between several credible sources.

Practice
Critical Thinking

Do you ever agree or disagree with the author of something you've read? As a reader, you should consider the author's purpose for the text. Is the author trying to persuade you in some way? Do you think that the author's information is based on fact? Readers should always examine the intent of the text they are reading. That's called *critical reading*, and it's another important strategic tool you should use when you read.

3. Timeliness. Check the date on the material. Some articles stay on the Web for years, so you will want to make sure that you are looking at current information. Do the links work, or are they broken? If the material is not timely, search for something more current.

4. Objectivity. It can be difficult to determine whether an organization is presenting material objectively. Language is one indicator—words like *obviously* and words that show strong emotion are signs that the writer is biased and not objective. We tend to rely on reputation or brand as a means of determining objectivity, as well. If a particular news source is known for being objective, more people will trust its information.

Digital Text Features

Digital text often includes features that can make reading it more fun than reading print. Hyperlinks can send you to another Web page or provide you with an image or information about the word or phrase you clicked on. When you move your cursor over a hot spot, you may be able to enlarge an image and see greater detail. Audiovisual features can enhance your reading by letting you hear the pronunciation of a word, listen to samples of conflict resolution dialogues, or watch a dental procedure being performed.

Online Dictionaries

A dictionary is an alphabetical list of words and their meanings, sometimes including a thesaurus section, which is a list of synonyms and antonyms related to the word. A thesaurus is also available as a stand-alone reference work. Many kinds of dictionaries can be found on a library shelf: general-purpose dictionaries, foreign language dictionaries, bilingual dictionaries, slang dictionaries, rhyming dictionaries, special subject dictionaries (medical, technical, law, etc.).

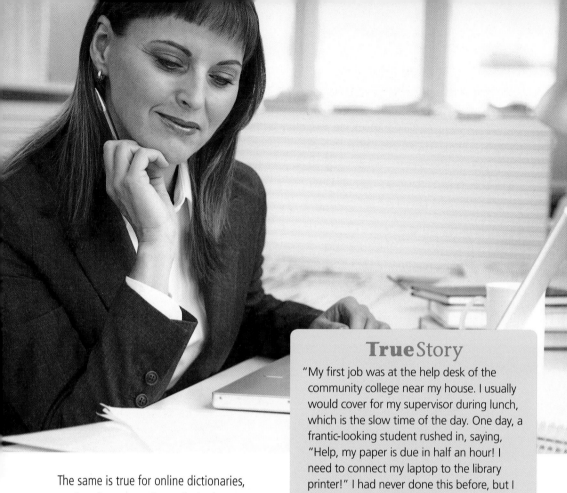

The same is true for online dictionaries, except that the content is not limited to a set number of pages. Speed is an advantage with online dictionaries: You can search for words quickly and effortlessly. Just type in a word in the search box, and within seconds you have the meaning of the word, without having to scan through printed pages. You may also have links to additional information, such as audio pronunciation. This is helpful when you come across a word in print and you don't know how it's pronounced. Some dictionaries feature illustrations or pictures to support the meaning of the word. As with other Internet sources, however, you should evaluate the dependability of the source; some dictionaries are open, meaning that users can go in and edit content. Here are a few online reference sites you might like to try:

dictionary.com This online dictionary includes entries from American Heritage, Random House, and Merriam-Webster. From here you can link to a thesaurus, flashcards, crossword puzzles, interesting quotes, and other language sites.

merriam-webster.com This is based on the print version of the Merriam-Webster dictionary. From this site you can link to a thesaurus, a Spanish-English dictionary, and a medical dictionary, as well as word games, word of the day, and videos. Also worth exploring is **visual. merriam-webster.com,** which contains thousands of images.

oxforddictionaries.com The Oxford English Dictionary (OED) is considered the premier dictionary of the English language. Choose from the free version or the paid subscription version. For general purposes, the free version is adequate. You can also choose from U.S. English or World English, plus educational features to improve your writing.

Final Thoughts About Online Reading

Before the digital era, people relied on printed reference materials for information. Printed materials can still be good resources, but keep in mind that they become outdated. An advantage to Internet-based reference materials is that they can be updated easily. Other advantages are their convenience and their interactive features. Some sources, such as newspaper articles, are available in both print and digital format. Whether you read print or digital format, remember to be a critical reader: Content is subject to question. Be skeptical of what you read, unless you are certain that the source is reliable.

Responding to What You Read

It is a good idea to keep a reading journal of your course reading, with added comments and analyses. Any notebook will suffice, or, if you are technologically inclined, use an electronic file. No matter what format you choose, use your journal to record the title of what you read, the main ideas, quotations from the text, and your own reflections on the material. There is no standard for what a reading journal should look like, but you might want to include the following pieces of information:

Create a summary. If you are reading a textbook or manual, note that units are often summarized at the beginning or at the end of each unit.

Questions? Sometimes what you read leaves unanswered questions that might lead you to research the material further or ask your instructor for clarification.

Write a personal response. Capture your impressions of why the text is (or is not) important and what the author is trying to say. Record any thoughts, arguments, or feelings about what you have read.

Unit Summary

- Pre-reading strategies, such as viewing the pictures and reviewing the boldface terms, help you build the scaffolding that will enable you to remember what you read.

- Strategies used during reading, such as finding the main idea, asking questions, outlining, and summarizing, promote reading comprehension and retention.

- Graphic organizers are especially useful tools for difficult reading.

- Whether you're reading print or digital text, read critically and be aware of the author's stance.

- Keep a reading log to capture your responses to what you've read.

Important Terms

How well do you know these terms? Look them up in the glossary if you need help remembering them.

pre-reading

scaffolding

skimming

main idea

graphic organizer

outline

summary

scanning

bias

Exercises

1. Choose a story in a newspaper, either print or online. Set a purpose for reading by changing the title of the story into a question. Ask a question beginning with *who, what, where, when,* or *how.* Note the information that the printed story didn't cover but that you'd like to know.

2. Read the following paragraph, and identify the main idea.

   > If you have been diagnosed with hypertension, or high blood pressure, it is possible to lower your blood pressure by making lifestyle changes rather than taking prescription medications. Losing weight, exercising regularly (at least 30 minutes a day), and eating a healthy low-sodium diet can bring your blood pressure down. Other heart-healthy changes include quitting smoking and limiting alcohol consumption (to one drink a day for women and two for men).

   Summarize the paragraph in your own words.

3. Use a search engine to find smart phone consumer reviews on the Internet. Make a list of five specific sources, with a brief explanation of the domain type (retail supplier, opinion, news story, university extension, manufacturer, etc.). Next, go to an online library or other research center, and perform another search. Find five more specific sources, and add them to your list. From all your sources, list the titles of the URLs that seem the most reputable.

4. Explore one or all of the online reference sites mentioned previously. Which site appealed the most to you? Why? Which interactive features were you already familiar with? What features surprised you? Record your reflections in a reading log.

Note Taking

KEYS TO
success

Identifying types of notes

Using technology to take notes

Taking notes in a variety of environments

Cognitive scientists have shown that we forget much of what we hear in class. However, students who take notes dramatically improve their ability to organize and remember important statements from lectures.[1] Taking notes helps you remember material and organize your thoughts in a variety of situations, not only in school but at work as well. In school, your notes will help you remember your reading or the key points made in class. At work, your notes will most likely communicate information to someone else. In some situations, such as when notes are for a patient's record or an inmate's file, the notes will tell another professional how a particular incident has been handled. In these cases, inaccurate notes can have dangerous consequences. In this unit, we will discuss how to take excellent notes so that you always communicate clearly.

[1] Einstein, G.O., Morris, J., & Smith, S. (1985). Note-taking, individual differences, and memory for lecture information. *Journal of Educational Psychology*, 77(5), 522–532. doi: 10.1037/0022-0663.77.5.522.

Types of Notes: Several Approaches

The ability to take purposeful notes is very valuable. There are many ways to take notes, and the key is to find the one that works for you. Read about a few note-taking systems and choose one for you.

Annotating Reading Material

Annotating is an important skill for improving reading comprehension and retention, or understanding and remembering what you read. When you make notes about your impressions and ideas or jot down questions in the margins, reading becomes an active process that takes you deeper into the material. Annotating is useful when you are reading for information found in textbooks, manuals, and study guides, but it goes without saying: *do not* write in books that don't belong to you! Future readers of the text may not appreciate your marginalia (margin notes). Here are the key steps in annotating:

1. Prepare to annotate. If you are using an e-reader, get to know the highlighting and annotation features on the device. You can highlight, circle text, add sticky notes, and even drag and drop text or graphics from the textbook into your notes. Knowing these features will help make annotating an easier and more productive process. If you are using a physical textbook that belongs to you, gather highlighters, pens or pencils, and sticky notes.

2. Read the first paragraph and highlight the main idea. The main idea is usually a single sentence that effectively sums up what the passage is saying. Do this for each paragraph. Then read over the highlighted main ideas. Write a short summary in the margins or on a sticky note.

3. Circle the main words or phrases that the passage discusses. These words can include key terms, glossary words, or words that are related to the main idea. This is especially helpful when you are reviewing the passage before an exam.

4. Make notes to yourself in the margins as you read. If you have a question or comment, write it next to the paragraph it applies to. Write a question mark (?) above words that are unfamiliar, and look up their definitions.

5. Mark any confusing parts of the reading that you need to go back and reread.

Do the same for each page, but be careful not to write so many notes on a page that it becomes difficult to read. Try using different colors for specific purposes. When you study, you will be glad you took the time to annotate.

Formatting Your Notes

Annotating involves taking notes right on your reading material. One advantage to this note-taking method is that all the information—original text and notes—is together on a book page or a handout. Although writing in textbooks is the norm for many people, others believe that writing in a book is disrespectful; it may also lower its resale value. If you can't bring yourself to write in a book, here are some nondefacing ways of taking notes.

Outlining. As you learned earlier, a standard outline contains Roman and Arabic numerals and uppercase and lowercase letters to arrange ideas, details, and examples in ordered groups. Outlines work well when you are reading textbooks, manuals, and study guides. For example, if you read a passage about blood and its characteristics, it could be presented in outline form. See Figure 7.1.

Pyramid Notes. Pyramid notes follow a similar approach as outlines. This simple note-taking strategy allows you to analyze your reading in an orderly manner. Pyramid notes are effective when you are reading for information in textbooks, manuals, or study guides. The top-to-bottom method creates a visual pyramid that breaks down the subject, main idea, and supporting details. It is then simple to summarize, synthesize, respond, or reflect upon your reading. The following steps describe how to employ this note-taking strategy.

I. Blood composed of red blood cells, white blood cells, platelets, and plasma

II. Red blood cells (Erythrocytes)

   A. Transport oxygen used in aerobic respiration

   B. Carry away CO_2 wastes

III. White blood cells (Leukocytes)

   A. Daily housekeeping and defense

     1. In tissues

       a. target damaged or dead cells

     2. In lymph nodes and spleen

       a. produce armies of cells

       b. battle viruses, bacteria, and other invaders

   B. Come from stem cells in bone marrow

IV. Platelets (Thrombocytes)

   A. Are colorless fragments in blood

   B. Band together with other substances during blood loss

     1. Coagulation

     2. Clotting

     3. Scab forms over wound

Figure 7.1 Sample outline

1. Write the subject of your reading at the center and top of a sheet of paper.

2. Beneath the subject, write the main idea. This is what the author is saying about the subject.

3. List the supporting details in columns under the main idea. In most texts, there will be at least three supporting details. Look for examples or quotations that effectively illustrate the main idea.

The following pyramid notes were written about a biology book chapter about blood.

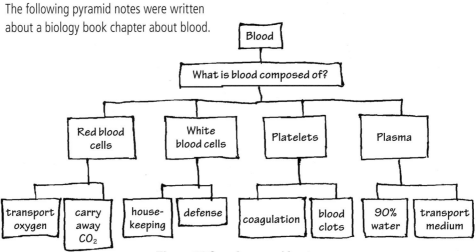

Figure 7.2 Sample pyramid notes

Mind Mapping. Pyramid notes and outlining are good for taking notes of reading material, but these formats probably are not the best for taking classroom notes. Pyramids and outlines work for information that is hierarchical, or grouped in a certain order. Textbooks and manuals usually present information in a hierarchical manner. In the classroom, however, the information often isn't presented in a certain order. In fact, the instructor may jump from one topic to another. Also, many times discussions and brainstorming are going on in the classroom, and discussions are often not presented in order, either. A mind map or concept map (which could also work for taking reading notes) is a particularly good way to visually link ideas that come up in the classroom. The central idea is positioned in the center, with the supporting ideas branching out from there. A mind map can easily be done using pen and paper, but see Figure 7.3 for an example of a digital mind map.

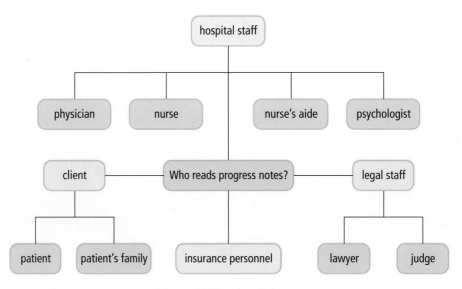

Figure 7.3 Sample mind map

Charting. Mind mapping works for organizing information in a relationship format, or in a way that shows how information is connected. For organizing information in chronological or time order, a chart is a great tool. In the nursing field, charts are used extensively to document patient information in discharge notes, plan of care, admission notes, and **progress notes,** which record the progress or changes in a person or situation over a period of time. In other careers, charts may be used to document the status of a work order or to document goals and outcomes. When creating a chart, consider whether the information is for your eyes only, or if someone else will be relying on your information. Legibility and accuracy are important in either case.

Note-Taking Tools

What should you use to take notes? Many people swear by pen and pencil, spiral-bound notebooks, steno pads, or note cards. People who enjoy using digital tools have a world of options to play with; more about that in the next section. For now, read on to learn more about resources for pen and paper note taking.

Notebooks. Most people use a different notebook for each topic. A common way to organize notes in a spiral-bound notebook is in a three-column format. In the left column, write the topic. In the middle column, record important quotes, paraphrase information, summarize key points, and write personal reflections. In the right column, record references, such as a page number or URL.

Steno Pads. Another paper option is a steno pad, originally designed for stenographers who use shorthand, which is a coded form of note taking. The steno pad flips over the top instead of side to side, a feature that works well for left-handed people. The trim steno pad fits neatly inside a bag or tote. Steno pads also have a subtle vertical rule on each page that

creates two columns. Stenographers have to take notes very quickly and under pressure. So, they fill up the left column before continuing to the right because it takes longer to drag your hand all the way across the page than it does to drag it halfway across the page. Even if you are not a stenographer, you can use the two-column format in many ways:

pros	cons
client name	**information**
goal	**outcome**
word	**definition**

Note Cards. Note cards provide the same features as a steno pad, but in a different format: front and back instead of side by side. And note cards are even more portable than steno pads. Taking notes on 3 x 5 index cards works well if you are researching a topic. Use a separate note card for each source. On the front of the card, record the source information, including page number and title or work. On the back, compile your notes from the source, whether it is a quote, paraphrase, or summary. You can organize your cards by source or by topic, or in any way that works for you.

No matter which paper method you choose, it is important to know who will read your notes. Most paper notes are read by only the note taker—you! However, keep in mind that in a professional setting, other people may need to look at your notes. Make sure they are legible and easy to follow. One way to ensure that notes are easy to read is to use technology to convert handwritten notes or even to create notes. The next section discusses the digital options for note taking.

Using Technology to Take Notes

Traditional handwritten notes using note-books, steno pads, or note cards work very well for many people. Note taking with pen and paper is tactile, involving touch, which many people believe aids in memory retention. Furthermore, you can format handwritten notes in any way that suits you at that moment. Still, you may find that digital note taking opens up a whole new world of information organization and makes you more productive. Today, many people are faster on a keyboard than they are with pen and paper.

Digital Note Taking

There are other reasons to consider digital note taking. Most note-taking applications, like Ever-note and OneNote, are supported by multiple platforms, such as laptops and smart phones. Digital notes can be indexed, or organized in a certain way, and are searchable, so you can find notes quickly and easily. You can easily import classroom slides or other materials into your notes. Perhaps the biggest bonus to using digital notes is that some note-taking applications are Web-based, which means you can access your notes anywhere, from any computer that has Internet access.

Be careful, however, of using laptops and other digital devices for anything other than taking notes. With digital devices, it's easy to veer off task and get sucked into the distracting world of social networking. Some instructors won't allow digital devices in their classrooms precisely for this reason. If you do use a digital device to take notes, be considerate. You'll distract others who sit near you if you are constantly checking email or scrolling through your Facebook page.

Can't decide between paper and digital? Use both. Scan your paper notes at the end of the day into a permanent electronic file. Or take notes on a tablet PC. It requires extra time, but keyboarding your handwritten notes into an electronic file gives you the opportunity to clean up, expand, and reflect on what you've written.

Using Audio Recordings

It's easy to see how digital devices enhance note taking. An audio recorder is another tool to consider when you must take notes on a difficult or complicated topic, or when you need to capture quotes **verbatim,** or word for word, such as at a conference or lecture. Small digital recorders and recording features on laptops make it easy to record conversations and lectures, but a word of caution: make sure you have permission to do so. If you do record, don't be tempted to just sit back while the recorder does all the work. Technology has been known to fail, so it's good practice to listen and take good notes, regarding the recorder as a backup. Audio recordings are particularly helpful for revisiting information. You can listen to the recording many times and then summarize the information in your own words. You also can record your own thoughts as you read and then listen to the recording later to organize your ideas and questions.

Audio recordings are commonly used in the workplace as well, mostly to protect company interests and employees. IT help desks and customer care centers often monitor calls for quality and training purposes. Health professionals may use voice-activated devices to record patient progress as they go from room to room. Then the information is downloaded as an mp3 file to be transcribed, or recorded in a print format, using a variety of note-taking strategies.

Collaborative Note Taking

Up to this point, all our note-taking strategies have involved just one note taker—you—making the note-taking experience quite personal. However, collaborative note taking elevates note taking to a new level. It involves a group of peers sharing their individual notes by posting them in one location that everyone in the group can access. Each member of the group has the opportunity to consider ideas through the different viewpoints and methods of the others.

Collaboration happens when people work together to reach a common goal. For true collaboration to take place, a group should be restricted to two or three people. If there are more than three people, it is difficult to keep track of everyone, and there may be too many ideas and opinions for successful sharing. Collaborative notes are useful in a variety of situations. In one scenario, a group of classmates may decide to take collaborative notes to understand a difficult class better. What one person didn't catch, another one probably did. In this situation, the three are approaching the same content with different perspectives, or viewpoints. In another instance, a group of co-workers may collaborate during a conference, each attending a separate workshop or session, and then meeting to share what they learned. In this situation, because three people can't all be in the same place at the same time,

the three co-workers pool their knowledge. You can probably think of other situations for collaboration. Here are some tips for taking collaborative notes:

- Choose the right tool. Consider each member's note-taking style. If everyone is digitally inclined, consider a note-taking application such as OneNote.
- Agree on formatting issues such as fonts, bullets, or numbering. The goal is to have consistency in how notes are taken so that everyone can understand them.
- In a classroom setting, assign a role to each person in the group. One person can take traditional classroom notes in an outline format. Another can present notes in a mind map. A third member can formulate possible multiple-choice questions to support the lesson.
- Evaluate one another's notes. Can they be made better? Which format was most helpful?
- Consider using an online tool, such as Google docs, or creating a wiki, which allows users to log in, share, edit, and discuss notes.

Collaborative note taking is successful only when all members contribute equally toward the common goal: to help one another learn. They must all be cooperative, communicative, and considerate. These traits are key to working well with others in school and in many other environments.

Taking Notes in a Variety of Environments

Just as you identify a purpose for reading, you should identify a purpose for taking notes. You may be taking notes in a variety of environments, and each note-taking situation will be approached differently. Who will read your notes? Are your notes for your own benefit, to help you review information? Or are you taking notes to fulfill work obligations? Will the information be delivered to you over the phone or in person? These are all points to consider as you approach your note-taking tasks. Here are some note-taking situations you may encounter.

Taking Notes Over the Phone

Businesses are often full of hustle and bustle: people coming and going, the phone constantly ringing as callers search for those who are unavailable. That's why it's important to take accurate notes over the phone. Sometimes the note taker will be writing down routine information, such as name, phone number, and a brief message. At other times, the note taker will be noting more detailed information, such as summarizing a customer's order or describing the nature of a technical problem. Here are some suggestions for effective phone communication:

- Confirm the caller's identity. Make sure you know who is calling.
- Verify spelling of the caller's name as well as any other unfamiliar words.
- Listen actively and take detailed notes.
- Verify all numbers, especially phone numbers or credit card numbers.
- Repeat information; allow the caller to confirm or correct information.
- Tell the caller what you will do with the message, but don't make empty promises such as "He will call you right back." Say instead, "I will give Dr. Centena this message right away."

TrueStory

"As a medical receptionist, one of my duties is taking phone messages for the medical staff. One day, a patient named David Yi called with an urgent message. He was having an allergic reaction to a recently prescribed medication. I saw that there were three patients with the same name, so I asked Mr. Yi for his date of birth and address to confirm his identity. When I was certain I had the right patient, I carefully wrote down his message and repeated it back to him. Only then did I feel confident enough to relay the message immediately to the doctor. So much could have gone wrong during this phone conversation; that's why I listen actively and take detailed notes."

Taking Classroom Notes

When you take notes over the phone, the resulting notes are usually for someone else's use, so accuracy is key. Taking classroom notes is similar in that you are capturing verbally delivered information. One difference is that classroom notes are for your benefit. Another major difference is that the instructor is sharing much more information than what is contained in a phone message: a flood rather than a splash. How do you keep from drowning in all that information?

Knowing how to take good classroom notes is important because you can't possibly catch everything your instructor says. You'll be so busy trying to write down everything, that you won't pay attention to what is actually being said. Imagine trying to read through all that material at test time, trying to decide what's important and what's not. Clearly written, accurate notes will help you review later on, and the physical act of writing down the notes will help you focus during class. Some people believe that note taking comes naturally, but here are some strategies you can use to become a better note taker:

- Read your assignment ahead of time. This classroom session should not be your first exposure to the material.
- Keep your notes neat and organized, preferably with each topic in its own spiral-bound notebook or steno pad or in one digital note-taking tool.
- Begin each note-taking session with a clean sheet of paper or with a new digital file. Write the date at the top.
- Note only the main ideas your instructor says; it is not necessary to write down everything.
- Don't use complete sentences. In other words, "include psych eval." Using shortened words will help you take notes more quickly.

- Use the margin (or right column of a steno pad or digital file) to record any questions that occur to you. You can ask your instructor later, or you can research them yourself.
- Use symbols, abbreviations, and shorthand, but make sure you remember what your shortcuts mean. Here are some common abbreviations you might consider:

Abbreviation	What it means
w	with
w/o	without
sth	something
s/o	someone
b/c	because
esp	especially
re	regarding
btwn	between
e.g.	for example
+ *or* &	and
>	greater than or better than

Figure 7.4 Common abbreviations

In addition to using strategies that help you take notes quickly and accurately, remember that the goal of notes is to summarize the material you are learning. Just as you summarize when you read text, you also summarize information that you hear, such as in the classroom. Remember that you are not just listing the main ideas of what you hear; you are also synthesizing the information, or gathering the information to form the main message of the lesson. Summarizing is an important strategy because it helps you not only remember what you hear in the classroom but also understand it.

Before the Meeting. Gather as much information as you can. Who are the attendees? What is the purpose of the meeting? Who is conducting the meeting? Decide how you will record your minutes. Consider which note-taking method you will use. Will you use pen and paper or type on a laptop? Can the meeting be audio recorded?

During the Meeting. As people enter the meeting room, check their names off the attendee list. Make yourself comfortable, and make sure you can hear everyone. Don't try to record every word that everyone says. Don't be afraid to ask, "Excuse me, but will you repeat what you just said?" Making people aware of your presence will remind them to speak clearly and take turns.

After the Meeting. Post-process your notes while they are fresh. In other words, review them and add additional comments. Clarify anything you didn't understand. Type your minutes accurately, and ask the meeting leader to proofread. Give the minutes a final check; when everything looks good, email a copy of the document to each attendee. Ask for feedback by a certain deadline, incorporate any corrections, and store the minutes in a central location.

Remember that meeting minutes are meant for other people to read, often at a later date, and in some careers, meeting minutes can be considered legal documents. In this way, meeting minutes are very similar to progress notes and notes taken by shift workers.

Taking Meeting Minutes

The system of Gregg Shorthand, invented by John Robert Gregg (1867–1948), was used extensively in business offices until the 1980s, and is still used in some offices today. This is a phonetic system, meaning that only the sounds of words, not the spelling, are recorded. Secretaries or stenographers relied on shorthand to take meeting **minutes,** which is a record of what was said in a meeting. It was important to transcribe the minutes immediately after the meeting, for shorthand is difficult to translate if done at a later time. Today, any meeting attendee may be asked to take minutes and may use any abbreviated or speedwriting system he or she likes—as long as it can be read back. Meeting minutes are important because they capture important discussions and decisions made in business, government, and nonprofit sectors. As with classroom lectures, meeting minutes should contain only the most important information. Here are some guidelines to help you record minutes:

> ## Practice
> ### Critical Thinking
> Think of how writing in a social media environment, say in the limited space of a Facebook status or a 140-character tweet, is similar to taking notes for others.

Taking Shift Notes or Progress Notes

As with meeting minutes, **shift notes** or progress notes are a record of information to be read by others. Shift notes include information to be read by staff beginning a new shift. Care must be taken when using abbreviations because others reading the notes may not understand your shorthand. Information must be descriptive and specific, including times and dates. For example, in this security record, the second-shift security guard is alerting the third-shift guard to a situation he encountered

Progress notes, also presented in chart format, are used by professionals such as patient care assistants, dental assistants, correctional officers, and help desk technicians. Progress notes are dated, and signed observations or summaries are used whenever a person or situation must be monitored over time. These types of notes become official records, and are often legal records, so note takers must use pen. Pencil notes can be erased and changed, which is not the purpose of ongoing progress notes.

For example, in the health care career, progress notes document a patient's care, and they are an important part of a patient's permanent medical record. Co-workers, hospital staff, clients, legal staff, and insurance personnel may read these notes. Because many people may be reading these notes, it is very important for notes to be descriptive, clear, and accurate.

> **True**Story
>
> "As an oral hygienist, I use my notes to encourage behavior change. One patient, Rachel, did not floss regularly, and I could see how it was affecting her health. So, I told her I was taking notes, and we would compare the results at her next visit. Six months later, her numbers were much better, and we were both excited. Now she's on her way to better oral health."

Date and Time	Observation	Follow-Up	Guard Initials
4/16/12 3:30 p.m.	3:30 pm: Heard noise from pool area. 2 females and 2 males (about 20 yrs old) had entered through unlocked gate. Told them this was private property and I would escort them out. They cooperated. I escorted them out at 3:45.	4:15 p.m. I locked the swimming pool gate. Trespassers have not returned.	J.L.
4/16/12 5:00 p.m.	Swimming pool is clear. No people are using it.	5:15 p.m. Checked gate, and it is still locked.	M.P.

Figure 7.5 Sample shift notes

Final Thoughts on Note Taking

Regardless of the type of notes you take or the format you use, notes are an important form of communication. In fact, it's one of the most useful skills you can master, both academically and professionally. In academic life, notes are a crucial part of learning new information. Notes can also help you make connections to what you already know. These connections help you reach a deeper level of understanding.

In the workplace, your notes serve as reminders to yourself. They help you to organize tasks, and capture information to help you make important decisions. And your notes are not just for you; they are useful documents for coworkers, too. Because notes are often meant to be shared, knowing who will read your notes can help you choose the type and format for your note-taking. There are many to choose from. Explore the different note-taking strategies presented here, and note taking will soon become second nature to you!

Unit Summary

- There are several types of notes, including notes written directly on the reading material or notes written on a separate sheet of paper.

- Pyramid notes and outlining present information in a hierarchical format.

- A mind map or concept map presents information in a relationship format.

- Pen and paper or digital devices are equally effective for taking notes. Choose the medium you are most comfortable with.

- Collaborative note taking allows concepts to be considered through various perspectives and approaches.

- Taking classroom notes, meeting minutes, and phone messages requires active listening.

- To save time when writing notes, use abbreviations, symbols, and incomplete sentences.

- Shift notes or progress notes intended to be read by others in the future present information in chronological or time order.

- Consider your audience. Are you taking notes for yourself or for others?

Important Terms

How well do you know these terms? Look them up in the glossary if you need help remembering them.

annotating	pyramid notes	outlining
mind mapping	charting	steno pad
digital device	verbatim	collaboration
minutes	shift notes	progress notes

Exercises

1. Choose an interesting story from an online magazine and print it out. Annotate the article in the margin, using a variety of tools such as highlighter, pen, pencil, and sticky notes.

2. Read the following passage.

> Technology makes it possible for employers to monitor their employees' every move, but how far can they go without infringing on privacy? Unless company policy states otherwise, your employer does indeed have the right to monitor your communications, including telephone conversations, voice mails, emails, and Internet use. This includes time spent surfing the Web, shopping online, or checking social networking sites. As an employee, assume that all company-owned devices are subject to monitoring, and that information gathered from such monitoring may be used during performance reviews.

   Without looking back at the passage, create a handwritten or digital mind map of everything you can remember.

3. Consider these three listening activities: listening to a song on the radio; listening to a news broadcast; listening to a friend describe a frightening experience. If you had to take notes to capture the main points of each scenario, which note-taking method or format would you choose for each scenario, and why?

4. Research several digital note-taking tools or applications. Which one are you familiar with? Which one would you like to try? When would you try it? Note your reflections in a notebook or in a digital document.

5. Look at the list of abbreviations in this chapter. Add your own abbreviations in a notebook or digitally.

UNIT 8

Writing Strategies

KEYS TO
success

Writing for different purposes
_____

Addressing different audiences
_____

Writing structures and organization
_____

Using appropriate language/style

it may seem like writing is a thing of the past. In today's world, we text and status and tweet, but we don't do much longhand writing. In fact, in a push to create computer-literate children, more and more elementary schools have abandoned penmanship in favor of keyboarding skills. However, even though the ways in which we communicate are changing, writing is still a critical part of most important transactions. If you want to buy a house, tell your life story, close a deal, make a contract, sue someone, pitch a proposal to your boss, appeal for insurance coverage for a special medical procedure, or even make a treaty between two countries, you will need to communicate your thoughts clearly in writing. Although your writing may not make the difference between war and peace, it could well determine whether you get the job . . . and in some careers, what you write could affect someone else's life in a huge way.

Strategy 1: Understand the Purposes for Writing

Before you start, you should ask yourself: "Why am I writing?" Knowing your purpose for writing will allow you to choose the language and structure that will lead to the response you expect from your reader.

Know the Purpose of Writing

Keep in mind that there can be more than one purpose for writing: an entertaining, engaging blog, for example, can certainly inform or persuade the reader as well. Most writing, however, begins with one main purpose. The three main purposes for writing anything are:

1. **To entertain.** Many people like to read for entertainment—they read to laugh, think, feel, and even cry. Not too long ago, it was almost exclusively professional writers who wrote to entertain with stories, books, and poems. Now, you too can write to entertain readers. You can email a joke to a friend or post a motivational quote to your status. If you are overflowing with inspiration and creativity, you can set up a blog: a publicly accessible web page where you can share stories, photos, or anything that you want to write. Blogs can cover common interest topics such as music, movies, and trends in fashion, or they can be geared for a specific audience. For example, nursing students may read a blog with inspirational thoughts about caring for patients, while help desk workers may enjoy blogs with funny stories about computer networking. Whether you write a story or a blog, writing to entertain is meant to be fun for the reader.

2. **To inform.** This is the most common purpose for writing in school. When you write a research paper, you write to provide information about your research topic. Writing to inform is also the most common form of writing used in business. If you've ever explained the dental coverage on composite fillings or outlined the steps in an IT procedure, then you know how to inform. When you write to inform, you communicate facts or observations to the reader. For example, a pharmacy technician may write about the side effects of a medication.

3. **To persuade.** In school or at work, you will sometimes write to express a viewpoint on an issue and try to convince your reader to agree. Maybe you want to persuade your patient to adopt better oral hygiene habits, or convince your co-workers of a new office procedure. This type of writing may be delivered in many ways, such as in an email, an essay, a memo, or even a lively poster.

One piece of persuasive writing, the cover letter, is especially important, since it may well determine whether you get the job. A cover letter is a business letter that is sent along with a resume. It is used to convince a potential employer that you fulfill the requirements for a job. A good cover letter does not simply summarize your accompanying resume. Your cover letter is an employer's first impression of you, and it provides a sample of your writing skills. The purpose of the cover letter is to persuade the hiring manager to interview and hire you for the open position.

Know the Audience for the Writing

Purpose and audience go hand in hand. In other words, once you know your purpose for writing, you have to think about your audience, the person or persons who will read what you write. For example, you know that the purpose of a cover letter is to persuade and that the audience is the potential employer. Identifying the purpose and audience before you write helps you plan and draft your writing. Here are some questions to ask before you start to write:

- **Who is the audience?** Your audience can range from one (friend, instructor, potential employer, or supervisor) to many (a public blog or an entry in a probation report). Consider your relationship with the audience. Another consideration: How well do you know this person or group? How much of yourself are you willing to reveal?
- **What does my audience need to know?** If you are writing for your peers—say, other dental assistants—you probably share common knowledge about your field. In that case, you do not need to explain the basic

principles of the subject. If, on the other hand, your audience is a dental patient, and you are writing instructions for oral hygiene care, the patient will appreciate a bit of background knowledge. In a cover letter, the audience (the potential employer) needs to know reasons for hiring this person.

- **What tone should I use to present my message to my audience?** When you are speaking, your voice conveys the tone to the listener. Your writing conveys tone, too, and it is important to choose the right tone. For example, if you were writing a text message to a friend, your tone can be chatty and friendly. You can write with abbreviations, emoticons, and incomplete sentences. But if you are writing a cover letter, you need to use a formal, serious tone. You want to make sure you use complete sentences, words that are spelled out, and correct punctuation. (Keep in mind that choosing the right tone applies to speaking as well. In an interview, you wouldn't want to use the same chatty tone you would use with friends.)

Your answers to these three questions will help you plan your writing so it says what you want it to say and in a way that matches the situation.

Strategy 2: Identify the Appropriate Writing Structures

Good writers use different writing structures, or ways of arranging information, to fit their purpose for writing.

Organization Depends on Purpose of Writing

Many times, the writing structure may be clear ("Summarize the seven elements of progress notes"), or you may need to decide on structure after you have identified the purpose for writing. The following structures are used for any writing purpose, both in school and in business.

Compare and Contrast. If your goal is to compare two or more things, you can structure your writing to state how the things are similar, or alike, and how they are different. For example, your first sentence could be something like, "A, B, and C are similar in some important ways, but there are also some key differences." See Figure 8.1 for an example of compare-and-contrast structure from a paragraph about heat transfer.

Cause and Effect or Problem/Solution. Sometimes you will need to explain why something happened, or you may need to describe a problem and how it was resolved. See Figure 8.2 for an example from an IT help desk report.

The first sentence describes what is similar.

Conduction, convection, and radiation all refer to ways that heat flows from one substance to another. Each of these transfers occurs in different ways.

This second sentence introduces the differences. The following paragraphs will discuss how the three methods of heat transfer differ.

Figure 8.1 Sample compare and contrast structure

Date and time of call	Caller name	Department	Extension	Resolved by	Date and time resolved
4/11/11 2:20 p.m.	D Nelson	Marketing	149	M Chavez	4/11/11 2:30 p.m.
Problem:	Unable to log into network or email on work computer.				
Solution:	Password was expired. Reassigned new password.				

Figure 8.2 Sample problem/solution structure

Sequence/Chronology. Sometimes you will need to arrange information **chronologically,** or in time order. For example, progress notes document a patient's care from the day of admission to the day of discharge. The information is given in sequence—the order in which it happened. The example below shows a security guard's log of events from the beginning of the shift to the end. The guard patrols the area every 30 minutes, and records the events of each patrol in order.

Security Firm:	Boulder Security
Post:	Main gate
Client name:	Pajaro Dunes Estates
Date/shift:	01/26/11 4:00 p.m. to midnight

Time	Condition	Officer	Report: yes/no	Report number
0400	On post. All secure.	Lopez	no	N/A
0430	Female trespasser enters premises on foot.	Lopez	yes	12–128
0500	No conditions to report.	Lopez	no	N/A

Figure 8.3 Sample sequence/chronology structure

Description. A description paints a picture, allowing the reader to experience what you—the writer—see, hear, taste, feel, and smell. This is a common form of writing that you will find in newspapers, magazines, incident reports, help desk logs, and patient progress notes. This descriptive and accurate observation about a hospital patient was taken by a medical assistant. It mentions precise units of time and measurements.

12:30 to 12:50: Patient ate ½ of lunch (all vegetables; no chicken or bread). She drank 50 mL of water. Looked pale. Said she was tired.

1:00: Patient rated pain a 6 and said she felt short of breath. Raised back of bed so she could sit up. Called dr. for pain medication orders.

1:10: Patient said she feels better after sitting up. Rated pain a 2. Cheeks pink, not pale. No meds given.

Figure 8.4 Sample description structure

Persuasion. Through persuasion, you attempt to convince a reader to accept your point of view. To convince readers that your viewpoint is the right one, you present facts (things that can be proven to be true) and opinions (what you think or feel about a topic). You can also compare and contrast to show how your viewpoint is better than another one. For example, people running for political office often compare themselves with their opponents, trying to show that they would do a better job. Persuasive writing is also useful when you want people to take action, like hiring you for a job.

Here is a cover letter written by someone who is applying for a job as a help desk specialist:

Alice Smith
17 Chestnut Street
Austin, TX 78759

June 6, 2011

Raul G. Ramirez
Women's and Children's Hospital
4505 Central Ave.
Austin, TX 78703

Dear Mr. Ramirez:

I am writing in response to your classified ad in the *Austin Citizen* for a Help Desk Specialist. My experience and education qualify me to fill this position.

I received my Associate's degree in information technology with a specialization in help desk administration in 2010, and for the past two years, I have been employed in the field of computer support, working first for Standard Corporate Catering Services, and then for American International Group. I have experience providing both telephone and walk-in support.

Women's and Children's Hospital serves a large, diverse community, and has been cited as one of the nation's leading medical centers. I would be proud to work for such an organization, and I look forward to the challenges and rewards of resolving computer support problems. I look forward to hearing from you to arrange a time when we can discuss my qualifications for this position. You can reach me at (618) 555-0991.

Sincerely,

Alice Smith
Enc.: resume

Figure 8.5 Sample cover letter

Here are some strategies for writing persuasively:

Make it direct. Using clear, concise points helps the reader understand what the problem is and what you want to happen. For example, if you write a letter asking for a replacement for a defective appliance, it is not a good idea to ramble on and on about why you are unhappy with the product and how upset you are. Use specific, short points such as "The oven does not heat up past 300 degrees. It also turns off unexpectedly. I would like a new oven or a refund."

Provide evidence. Replace generalities with specifics. For example, if you are writing an email to your boss asking to change your work schedule, you can include evidence that supports your goal of having more flexible work hours: "Two of the medical coders in another office have flextime and have increased the number of bills processed each day." Specific evidence is more convincing.

Share benefits. Remember that your goal in writing persuasively is to get something from someone else. In order to do that, you need to point out a benefit, or "what's in it for them." Say you want your childcare provider to extend pick-up times so that you don't have to leave work early to pick up your children. You could explain that having a later pick-up time means a less hectic end-of-day for the childcare provider because every parent won't be arriving at the same time.

Provide action steps. At the end of your writing, provide action steps. For example, if you write a letter to your apartment building manager asking for your plumbing to be repaired, state that you will call in two days to schedule an appointment.

Be firm, but polite. If you are upset about something, and want to write a letter or email to change the situation, it can be natural to feel angry and let that anger creep into your writing. But it is better to maintain politeness in persuasive writing because people are more willing to respond to calm, polite requests. On the other hand, don't be so polite that your persuasive argument disappears. Use the points above to make sure your request is considered seriously.

Summarize. When you summarize, you use your own words to express your understanding of a topic. Summaries are shorter versions of longer material. Often, instructors will ask you to include an opinion in a paragraph separate from the summary. Sometimes these pieces will be submitted to the instructor, and other times they will be shared with your peers through a discussion board.

A **discussion board** is intended to stimulate intellectual exchange when writers are separated by distance and time. It also provides a forum for students to ask and answer important questions about the course material. Discussion is formal, and your responses, in both content and writing style, should demonstrate thoughtful reflection and review. Here are some strategies to help foster a productive and lively digital learning community:

- Summarize your thoughts clearly, starting each paragraph with a clear statement.
- Demonstrate critical thinking in your post. If you give an opinion, state facts that support it. In the security guard example, the guard may write: *I believe the entrances need more lights to protect the building from trespassers who want to sneak into the pool area.* (This is the clear statement of opinion.) *Studies show that well-lit entrances prevent people from trespassing on community property at night.* (These are the facts to support the opinion.)
- Give thoughtful and complete responses to your classmates that are more than "I agree" or "Good idea." Just as you are looking for feedback from your peers, they are looking for quality feedback from you.
- Stay on topic, but feel free to expand on ideas.
- Take the discussion deeper by sharing work experience anecdotes or other outside resources.
- Improve learning by asking for responses and reflections from others. For example, discuss a related work issue on which you would like some feedback.
- Add context to your responses by restating someone else's comment: "So, what you're saying is ____. I agree, but I also think that ____."
- Proofread your postings, so they are free of spelling and grammatical errors.

Discussion boards allow time for thoughtful collaboration, since comments can be read carefully and revisited; furthermore, responses can be constructed carefully, with supporting evidence. It takes practice to do this well, so it is important to complete the unit reading first and then take

the time to carefully craft your discussion responses. In addition, be sure to review your responses before posting to the board. When you take the time to respectfully and fully explore a subject, you and your classmates will have a richer, more interesting learning experience.

Structure Choice and Paragraph Development

A paragraph is a collection of sentences related to one idea. Whatever writing structure you choose will influence how you develop your paragraphs. For example, in a compare-and-contrast piece, each paragraph should cover a similarity or a difference. A problem-and-solution structure offers a natural paragraph division: first discuss the problem and then devote a new paragraph to the solution. In a sequence/chronology structure, each paragraph can cover a specific segment of time. Description, persuasion, and summary lend themselves to the format of the general multiparagraph essay, which can be arranged as follows:

I. Introductory paragraph: gives background information and states main idea

II. Body: two or more paragraphs that support the main idea

III. Concluding paragraph: restates the main idea

Sometimes, you will need to write only a stand-alone paragraph, in which case it will be formatted much like a mini-essay, with three main parts: topic sentence, supporting sentences, and concluding sentence. See Figure 8.6 for a one-paragraph summary of a newspaper article about school gardens.

The topic sentence introduces the topic of school gardens.

In response to the national problem of childhood obesity, gardens are taking root in schools all over the country. Students and teachers sow, cultivate, and harvest vegetables in raised beds constructed by parents. School gardens promote healthy eating habits and teach children about nutrition. Children enjoy growing their own food and eating the fruits of their labor. School gardens are the perfect place to begin a lifelong journey of healthy eating.

Supporting sentences give details about the school gardens.

Concluding sentence restates the main idea or gives an opinion.

Figure 8.6 Sample one-paragraph summary

A topic sentence should be general enough so that supporting sentences are needed for explanation. If your topic sentence declares that school gardens are taking root all over the country, then a question will automatically pop into your reader's mind: Why are school gardens important? Your supporting sentences should answer this question. Your concluding sentence summarizes the information or gives your final thoughts on the subject.

Now that you understand the nuts and bolts of writing, you can focus on the aspects of writing that require a more personal touch: language and style.

Strategy 3: Attend to Language and Style

You've learned about planning your writing by identifying the purpose—the "why"—and the audience—the "who." You've also learned about the "what"—the structure of your writing. Although those things are very important in writing, there is something equally important to think about: the language and style.

Return to the Purpose and the Audience

Word choice is the rich and precise language that makes your writing informative and engaging to the reader. If you do not choose words carefully, you risk confusing or losing your readers. After all, how you write to your friend is very different from how you write to your instructor or colleagues. Your choice of words is determined by whether you are using a casual register or a formal register of language.

Very early on, you learned that certain situations call for different ways of communicating. You speak to your friends one way and to your instructors another way. You speak to your three-year-old niece differently from how you speak to a co-worker. What distinguishes these situations is not only word choice, but grammar, sentence length, and other language and social conventions. It is the same with writing. Certain situations call for different writing styles. Writing for academic and business settings calls for a **formal register,** which includes specific, purposeful word choices and complete sentences of varied lengths and structures. Formal register uses **Standard American English** (SAE). SAE follows the standard conventions, or rules, of English grammar, including punctuation, capitalization, sentence structure, and spelling. Formal register is socially careful and restrained.

TrueStory

"As a medical biller and coder, I am responsible for what goes out to the insurance companies. One day I found errors in the codes from our contract coder, and it wasn't the first time. I vented to Brian, my office mate: 'Sheesh! Look at this! Have we really been paying premium charges EVERY TIME the lab asks for them?!' Brian answered, 'Yeah, that's pretty crazy. You should tell Candace about it.' Knowing that email communication is often kept on record, I changed my wording to a more formal register. Here is my email to Candace, our supervisor: 'I have found some errors in the codes from our contractor. I think we should review all of her codes to be certain we do not have additional errors.'"

On the other hand, **casual register** is characterized by playful, coined (made-up) words, and incomplete sentences. We *all* use casual register with our friends and family. It's a way of showing that we belong. In casual register, we might use **slang,** the ever-changing, short-lived vocabulary of a particular group. Some examples are common American slang ("My car was totaled") and textspeak (lol, ttyl). Slang is best suited for informal speaking and writing situations, however. Just as you wouldn't show up for an important interview in jeans and flip flops, you wouldn't use casual register in academic or professional communications such as essays, business letters, reports, and contracts. Written language, in general, is more formal than spoken language, since it is permanent and subject to careful analysis. In order for your writing to be well received, choose the appropriate language register—casual or formal—for your audience.

Casual register comes quite naturally to most people, but many need to work at expressing themselves in a formal register. Several style guides exist, both print and online, to help you master the features of formal register. Your instructor may have suggestions, but some excellent style guides to have on hand are *The Gregg Reference Manual* and the *AP Stylebook* (print or online).

Another thing to think about as you choose words in your writing is your own personal, unique voice. **Voice** in writing is writing that "speaks" naturally on the page. How do you come across in your writing? Does your personality shine through? Do you sound friendly, inexperienced, authoritative, high energy, or professional? When you read your writing aloud, it should sound like you, with words and phrases that are appropriate for your experience, but in a tone that connects with the audience and satisfies the purpose for writing. You

reveal your voice through your choice of words and your sentence structure.

Letting your voice shine through makes your writing enjoyable to the reader, but an element that makes your writing easier to read is sentence fluency. Fluency refers to the way in which sentences flow effortlessly from one to the next, and from paragraph to paragraph. You can improve **sentence fluency** by using transition words, varying your sentence lengths, and varying your sentence types.

Practice
Critical Thinking

Make a vocabulary section in your phone or datebook, and add an entry at least every other day. In that section, analyze the vocabulary of at least one person: classmate, instructor, or other acquaintance. Listen carefully to the vocabulary your subject uses, and answer these questions: Is the person's language register appropriate to the topic and setting at hand? Can you use this person as a role model? Have you learned any words from this person?

Transition words show the relationship between ideas within sentences, from sentence to sentence, and from paragraph to paragraph. Figure 8.7 shows some common transition words according to type of writing.

In addition to using transition words, experiment with sentences of various types. Sentences that are all the same length or that start the same way make your reading sound choppy or uninteresting. There are four sentence types, as shown in Figure 8.8.

Type of Writing	Transition Words	Example
Compare/Contrast	likewise, similarly, on the other hand, nevertheless, but, however	Fluorescent lights, on the other hand, work in an entirely different way.
Sequence/Chronology	first, next, then, later, while, later on, as soon as, an hour later, meanwhile	First, make sure you have quit all applications. Then, turn off your machine.
Expository/Description	for example, for instance, also, suddenly, such as	Sometimes you will need to help patients describe symptoms. For example, you can ask whether pain is sharp or dull.
Restatement	in other words, that is, to put it differently	When making rounds, be sure that the perimeter of the building is secure. In other words, check all exits and entrances, including stairwells.

Figure 8.7 Transition words

Type of Sentence	Explanation	Example
Declarative	The sentence makes a statement; ends with a period.	Nursing is an excellent career for people who like to help others.
Interrogative	The sentence asks a question; ends with a question mark.	Is nursing a good career for people who like to help others?
Imperative	The sentence gives a command; ends with a period or exclamation point.	Help the man who fell. Help him now!
Exclamatory	The sentence shows strong emotion or feeling; ends with an exclamation point.	He fell and is badly hurt!

Figure 8.8 Types of sentences

Try including questions and exclamations in your writing, if doing so works with the purpose and audience. To add interest to your writing, you can also use sentences that are different lengths and that vary in sentence beginnings. For example, in the following, the second set of sentences means the same as the first, but is much more interesting to read:

- The man fell. His arm is bleeding. He is hurt. A doctor came. The man will get better.
- A repairman fell from a tall ladder! After he fell, it was clear that he hurt his arm because it was bleeding a lot. The man was badly hurt, but a doctor at the scene said the man will get better in time.

Now that you understand a few elements of style, see whether you can identify them in the following writing samples. As you read, take careful note of the voice. Is it friendly or professional? What about the language? Is it formal register or casual register? Are the sentences complete, and do they come in various lengths and complexities, with some being short and some long? Finally, consider the purpose of each writing sample and the likely audience.

The history of everyone's favorite dessert, ice cream, dates back to ancient times. The Roman Emperor Nero (CE 37–67) is reported to have ordered ice to be transported to Rome from the Apennines, a mountain range that runs the length of peninsular Italy, and more specifically, from the Corno Grande glacier. To transport the ice quickly and efficiently over great distances while maintaining its frozen condition was a logistic feat requiring ingenuity and engineering. Once the ice arrived in Rome, it was mixed with fruit toppings to create a rare and much coveted sweet treat.

Essay

Audience: Student to instructor

Voice: Scholarly, authoritative

Words/Structure: Formal register; complete and complex sentences

Purpose: To inform

May 5   12:00PM

Hey! Big Dipper open.
Free samples green tea
ice cream at 3! ttyl :-D

Text Message

Audience: Friend to friend

Voice: Casual, friendly

Words/Structure: Casual register; incomplete sentences; symbols; abbreviations

Purpose: To inform, entertain, and persuade

Frozen dairy desserts	
Avoid regular ice cream and premium frozen yogurt. Choose low-fat or non-fat ice cream (no more than 3 grams of fat per ½ cup serving).	

Plan of care

Audience: Nutritionist to patient

Voice: Professional, scientific

Words/Structure: formal register; simple; precise instructions

Purpose: To inform and persuade

Although the subject matter in all three examples is the same (ice cream), the intended audiences are different. Therefore, the register, the voice, and the sentence structure are different. The word *Hey*, the sentence fragment *Free samples green tea ice cream at 3*, the *ttyl* sign-off, and the "open smile" emoticon (:-D) are appropriate for text messages and emails among friends, but this textspeak is much too casual for school or work. On the other hand, your friend might find it strange if you suggest going for a scoop of a *much coveted sweet treat* or *premium frozen yogurt*. Remember: choose the appropriate language register for your audience.

Final Thoughts on Writing Strategies

Writing is never learned once and for all: it is an ongoing process that takes time and practice. In school and in the real world, you will be given a variety of writing tasks, some easy and quick, and others quite challenging, requiring research and reflection. Developing a sense of purpose and audience, in all types of communications, will help you identify the appropriate structure and language register to use in your writing. This is a challenging skill to develop, especially in a world of increasingly complex text types, language, and delivery methods. But as with many things, practice makes it an easier process.

Unit Summary

- Writing is a crucial form of communication.
- A writer can write for the purpose of entertaining, informing, or persuading.
- Blogs can be used to entertain a reader.
- The most common reason for writing is to inform, or educate.
- When you persuade, you try to convince a reader to agree with you.
- A cover letter is an important piece of persuasive writing.
- Knowing the audience helps you plan your writing.
- Different writing structures, such as compare/contrast, problem/solution, sequence, description, persuasion, and summary, help you organize your writing.

- Writing structure impacts paragraph development.
- Word choice is the rich and precise language that makes the writing piece informative and engaging.
- Voice is your individual writing style; it lets the reader "hear" you on the page.
- Sentence fluency refers to how sentences flow from one sentence to the next and from paragraph to paragraph.
- Transition words help sentences flow from one to the next.

Important Terms

How well do you know these terms? Look them up in the glossary if you need help remembering them.

writing to inform	summarizing	voice
writing to entertain	discussion board	formal register
writing to persuade	narrative	casual register
audience	expository	
blog	Standard American English	

Online Resources

www.bartleby.com/usage/

Associated Press Stylebook
apstylebook.com

Online Writing Lab (OWL) at Purdue University
owl.english.purdue.edu

Exercises

1. Consider the purpose of this unit on writing strategies. Is it to entertain, inform, or persuade? Do you think the writer had all three purposes in mind? Cite examples of word choice, voice, and sentence structure to support your response.

2. It is 20 years from now. You are in a meeting, and your manager is sharing your professional accomplishments with your peers. What is said?

3. The following security guard incident report, to be filed as evidence with a police report, uses casual register and slang, which are inappropriate for the intended purpose and audience. Rewrite it so it adheres to conventions of standard English, including word choice, punctuation, and sentence structure.

   > Dude. In the afternoon, I'm guessing @ 4:30, I saw this chick in a blue-colored vehicle coming at me, like, right toward the gate. I ain't lying. I jumped out the way to save my skin and then she swerved into the lot next to the guardhouse. Check it. She got out the car I told her to stop but she gave me the stink eye and kept on walking like nobody's business and when she got to the gate she crawled under the gate and started to run down the road toward the townhouses. Wasn't nobody here but me and I ain't seen where she went.

4. Go back to the section containing the three writing samples about ice cream. Read the concluding paragraph that compares and contrasts the three samples. What transition words are used to illustrate similarities and differences? Choose one of the ice cream writing samples and rewrite it for a different audience.

UNIT 9

Study Strategies

KEYS TO
success

Applying strengths and strategies to studying
_____
Overcoming habits that prevent successful studying
_____
Identifying studying resources around you
_____
Using reliable study strategies to create a routine

When it comes to studying for a test, it sometimes seems as if people fall into three groups. There are people who study and perform well. There are also people who do not take the time to study, but they take the test and do very well. Lastly, there are people who study the material so well that they know it inside and out, but their score on the test is terrible. It can be frustrating to study long and hard and then not succeed on a test. It can also be very easy to wonder why tests are so important. Why do instructors put so much weight on tests anyway? How will they apply to life outside of school?

In school, tests are important because they measure how well you understand the subject; instructors use tests as a check to make sure learning is happening. And believe it or not, testing will come into play in your life outside of school as well. Many careers involve periodic tests. For example, suppose you are working as a paralegal in a law firm or a corporation. In order to keep up with the licensing requirements of your job, you may have to take a qualifying exam in real estate law. You can improve your chance of passing the test by developing effective study strategies. A first step is to analyze your study habits. The next step is to build an effective study routine based on the strengths; this will help you correct the weaknesses. You'll be able to apply the study strategies you develop to your work in school and to other parts of your life as well.

Preparing for Academic Success

You know that succeeding in school requires hard work. In the past, you may have been disappointed when your efforts just weren't paying off in terms of good grades, making academic success seem like an unattainable goal. But here's a hint: it isn't just how you *work* that makes a difference, it's also how you *learn*. And everyone learns a little differently. Knowing how *you*, as an individual, learn has the potential to make studying a positive and rewarding experience.

Develop an Awareness of How You Learn

Each person has his or her own unique style of learning. There is no "one size fits all." For example, your friend may have discovered that the best way to prepare for an exam is by being part of a study group. On the other hand, you may prefer to review your notes in the privacy of your room or the quiet corner of a library. To figure out how you learn best, start by asking yourself some questions.

What academic strategies have worked in the past? Did a certain style of note taking make studying for an exam easier? Did recording lectures help you relax and pay attention in class because you knew you could listen to them again at home? Did setting a study schedule help you get through the material more efficiently? When you look back on your past experiences as a student, were you more likely to prefer a quiet room with few distractions? Or did you choose to study in a more public space with music playing and with people present?

What strategies, methods, or habits have not worked in the past? Identifying what doesn't work can be just as effective as discovering what does work. For example, if you've taken notes on a classroom lecture but then got home and realized you didn't know what your notes referred to, you might plan to use an audio recorder to record the next lecture. When you know which strategies are unsuccessful, you can avoid them in the future.

Which academic tasks did you like or dislike? Think about your past academic experiences. Which were relatively easy for you to accomplish and which required extra effort? For example, you might have enjoyed solving math problems but dreaded writing term papers.

When it came to taking tests, did you do better on multiple-choice questions but find essay exams more challenging? The answer to this question will help you plan ahead. You'll be able to spend less time on tasks that are easier for you, and focus most of your time on more challenging tasks.

What do you already know? Ask yourself about the subjects you are studying. What do you already know about them? How can this prior knowledge help you achieve success in your coursework? Think about the learning you have under your belt already, and apply it as you study new material.

What interferes with your studying? What things in your life prevent you from studying or make studying less effective? Are there too many **distractions,** or things that take your attention away from your studying? Maybe the TV is always on at home, or maybe you can't stop worrying about something at work, or you feel guilty for not spending time with your children. You can avoid distractions if you **prioritize,** or list things in order of how important they are. Once you know what your priorities are, you can plan your life so that when you need to study, studying is near the top of the list.

Asking yourself these kinds of questions will help you pinpoint your own unique learning style.

Three Learning Styles

Learning style refers to the way in which a person processes and integrates, or combines, new information with old information. Researchers in the field of education have identified a variety of learning styles. One widely used model distinguishes three main styles: visual, auditory, and kinesthetic. Learners enjoy these categories as organizing principles that explain their most preferred methods of learning; however, there is considerable debate about whether these "learning styles" actually explain real learning differences. What is important to remember is that, while you may discover that one of these styles is more suited to your needs and abilities, you can adopt other learning styles as well to improve upon your preferred style.

Visual learners. Visual learners process information more easily through the sense of sight. If you're a visual learner, you are likely to benefit from pictures, books, graphs, charts, videos, and other visual materials. A study tool like flashcards can give a significant boost to your academic performance. A traditional flashcard is an index card with important information written on one side. This information might be a key concept, a vocabulary word, a mathematical formula, one step in a process, etc. It can be expressed verbally or in the form of a picture or diagram. Flashcards are most effective when the information is short and succinct, or to the point, so it is easier to recall. Here are some study strategies for visual learners:

- Use flashcards (paper or digital).
- Make charts or diagrams to help you organize information. These can be made by hand on graph paper or on a computer using word processing software.
- Highlight key ideas or information in textbooks.

Auditory learners. Auditory learners rely more on their sense of hearing to absorb and retain new information. Whereas a visual learner may learn more from reading a textbook or watching a video, an auditory learner will benefit more from listening to a lecture or a podcast, for instance, or from discussing class work with fellow students.

These are some common study strategies for auditory learners:

- Take part in a study group.
- Use a digital audio recorder to record and play back lectures.
- Record notes and textbook information on your audio recorder.
- When studying by yourself, read out loud to help you retain information.

Kinesthetic learners. Kinesthetic learners take a hands-on approach to learning. If you're a kinesthetic learner, your sense of touch is key to successful learning. In the classroom, a kinesthetic learner learns best when the learning environment includes physical activity of one kind or another. In a course on heating and cooling systems, for example, a lecture on how to repair an air conditioner will be much less effective than actually doing the work. As a kinesthetic learner, you will probably learn more quickly by actually taking apart the air conditioner than by hearing about it. Here are some study strategies for kinesthetic learners:

- Take notes during your classes. Writing is a kinesthetic experience.
- Try to find ways to make the material tangible, or hands-on. This might involve making a three-dimensional model or a drawing of a key concept.
- Make the most of working in lab settings for science courses.
- If applicable, do field work to get first-hand experience of the subject you are studying.

Organize Yourself

Finding the time and place to do your best work is essential to being successful and reaching your goals. Are you more alert in the morning or the early evening? This will help you decide when you should schedule study time.

Make a study space. Make sure you have a place that is set up for studying with everything

Practice
Critical Thinking

A number of investigators have come up with different models for assessing a person's individual learning style. You can find free tests on the Internet, typically in the form of questionnaires. After you take a test, think about the results. Do they surprise you? Do you agree? Look for strategies that work well for your specific type of learning and think about changes you can make to help you succeed.

you need to have an effective study session, including your textbook, a notebook or note cards, and pen or pencil. You should also have a dictionary or access to an online dictionary. The area should be free of clutter. Nobody wants to waste a half hour of precious study time searching for a textbook—and if you sit in a cluttered room, you may think more about cleaning the place up than about studying. Ideally, your study space should also be free from distractions. Noisy children or a family member who wants your attention will make studying close to impossible. If there are too many distractions at home and you can't get away from them, the campus or community library is an option. On the other hand, you might find it difficult to concentrate in a relatively quiet environment. The background chatter of a coffee shop might be more suited to you, so long as you can politely turn away friends who might wander in and want to socialize. Try a few different types of environments for studying, and see where you get the most work done.

Make a study schedule. As you learned in Unit 4, time management is an important skill that helps you get organized and reduce stress. You know that creating a study schedule that takes the "big picture" into account is the first step. In addition to recording your class schedule, you can write down the significant academic dates for the entire semester. A quick glance at this calendar will tell you when important papers are due, when projects have to be completed, and when you'll be taking final exams. Having this information at your fingertips will help you plan ahead so you will have enough time to get your work done. You also learned in Unit 4 that your weekly schedule should include all of your commitments, whether social, work, personal, or academic. You know that prioritizing which activities are optional and which ones are nonnegotiable will help you stay on track.

Monday	Tuesday	Wednesday	Thursday	Friday
7–8:45 a.m. Breakfast Kids to school Walk to work*	7–8:45 a.m. Breakfast Kids to school Walk to work	7–8:45 a.m. Breakfast Kids to school Walk home	7–8:45 a.m. Breakfast Kids to school Walk to work	7–8:45 a.m. Breakfast Kids to school Walk home
9 a.m.–1 p.m. Work	9–1 p.m. Work	9–11 a.m. Study for test: review flashcards	9 a.m.–1 p.m. Work*	9–11 a.m. Study for test: review notes, key terms
1–2 p.m. Lunch with mom Walk to school	1–2 p.m. Bus to school (pack lunch) (Mom picking up kids)	11–12:30 p.m. Lunch with Lynn and Julia	1–2 p.m. Bus to school (pack lunch) (Mom picking up kids)	12–1 p.m. Bus to school (pack lunch) (Miguel picking up kids)
2 p.m. Pick up kids Walk home	2–4 p.m. School library: paper on genetics	12:30–2:00 p.m. Read chapters for class in library Walk to school	2–4 p.m. School library: paper on genetics	2–4 p.m. Class/TEST
3–4 p.m. Help kids with homework Start dinner	4–7 p.m. Class	2 p.m. Pick up kids Walk home	4–7 p.m. Class	4–5 p.m. Bus home
4–6 p.m. Study for skeletal and muscle test (Friday); skim notes	7–8 p.m. Bus home	3–4 p.m. Help kids with homework; start dinner	7–8 p.m. Bus home	5–6 p.m. Start dinner
6–7 p.m. Dinner	8–9 p.m. Kids bedtime	4–5 p.m. Get ready: school awards dinner Bring dessert Walk to school	8–9 p.m. Kids bedtime	6–7 p.m. Dinner
7–8 p.m. Family TV night	9–10 p.m. Dinner with Miguel	6–8 p.m. School dinner	9–10 p.m. Dinner with Miguel *Shift change next week: 9 a.m.–2 p.m.	7–9 p.m. Game night with neighbors 9–10 p.m. Kids bedtime Movie with Miguel
8–9 p.m. Kids bedtime		8–9 p.m. Kids bedtime		
9–10 p.m. Read chapter for class tomorrow		9–10 p.m. Write draft of paper on genetics		
* Walk ten miles this week				

Figure 9.1 Sample weekly calendar

Now estimate how much time you will need to prepare for each of your classes. In general, give yourself at least two hours of outside preparation for each hour of class time. Finally, write down on your weekly calendar which hours of the day you will devote to studying. Be specific. Instead of just noting "study," write down what you're studying during a given period of time. For example, "Study business accounting 4–6 p.m., Tuesday and Thursday." See Figure 9.1 for an example of a weekly calendar for a nursing student who works part-time as a receptionist at a doctor's office and has a family.

Manage your time. Combining school with work and family life can be daunting. Even the most carefully worked out schedule is only a plan. It is not an absolute blueprint for how to live your life. There will be times when you will need to close the books and be with friends or loved ones, or work that extra shift in order to save money for a trip or holiday shopping. Hopefully, these times will prove to be the exception and you will be able to strike a comfortable balance between studying and carrying on with the rest of your life. The following are some effective time management tips:

- Study at a regular time and in a regular place.
- Use free periods between classes to review your lecture notes.
- Do not devote more than two hours of study to one course at a time. To stay focused and maintain your concentration, take a break

after a two-hour block of time and then switch to another subject. You may find that you actually do better with more frequent breaks.
- Review your notes for each course on a weekly basis.
- Prioritize your study goals; make sure you've scheduled a greater amount of time for those subjects or assignments that require more work.

Maintain a Positive Attitude

Managing your time and organizing your study space will also help you manage stress and maintain a positive **attitude,** or your personal view on things. Having a positive attitude will go a long way toward helping you achieve academic success. As often as necessary, remind yourself that you are capable of handling whatever assignments you are given. Use positive affirmations to develop and strengthen a feeling of confidence in your abilities to succeed in your studies.

To a great degree, managing stress goes hand in hand with taking greater control of your life in order to meet the goals you have set for yourself. By maintaining a positive attitude as you pursue your goals, you will feel more in control of the demands in your life and be more successful. Your self-confidence will grow along with your chances of achieving academic success.

Using a Variety of Studying Resources

Your school campus and your community have many **resources** that you can use strategically to help your academic success. The Internet is also available and is a convenient resource for information and opportunities to learn from and with others studying the same topic. Knowing which resources are available and what each type offers is the key to getting the support you need when you need it.

Campus Resources

Every campus is unique, and the availability of resources differs from one to another. The following resources, however, can be found at most campuses.

Learning resource center. The campus library or learning resource center is an excellent resource for helping you improve academic success. You can investigate the resources and services available at your campus learning resource center between classes. You also can access all of the library's extensive databases online, making it convenient for you to study from anywhere. Your campus will have a staff member or librarian who can help you locate and use resources. Though each center is different, most centers will have a variety of resources including:

- Print materials such as books, periodicals, journals, trade magazines, research papers, reference materials, and newsletters
- Electronic materials such as online library catalogs of all of the print material available, videos, audio recordings, webinars, and databases, which are searchable lists of available resources
- Computer labs for writing papers and creating presentations
- Information on how to set up a study group or find a tutor and, if the center is in a physical building, meeting rooms
- Workshops or seminars on general academic strategies or specific subjects
- Access to academic and professional counselors

It is worth it to visit your campus learning resource center and take a tour with a staff member. The library is meant to offer you support outside the classroom and is an important part of the study resources available to you.

Instructors. Your instructors are another invaluable source of help and support. Their goal is to help you master the subject material, and since they are experts, they are ideal resources for support. Typically, instructors will meet with you outside of class hours. You can arrange to meet with your instructors in person by setting up an appointment beforehand. You might also correspond with them via email when you want clarification about an assignment, for instance, or when you need supplemental instruction.

Peer academic coach. Similar to tutors, peer coaches are students who offer support and guidance to fellow students. At some schools, professional learning specialists supervise peer coaches. The services they offer may be available on a walk-in basis at a campus location or by appointment. For example, you may be able to contact a peer coach through the campus learning resource center. Explain your particular interests and needs and how the coach can

help you improve academic success. In general, however, coaches are prepared to offer guidance in the following areas:

- Effective study techniques
- Managing time and energy
- Reading strategies and concentration
- Note taking and preparing for tests
- Test taking and stress reduction tips

Study groups. What if your school doesn't offer peer academic coaching but you still want the support of other students? If that's the case, you might want to start a study group or join one that's already up and running. Study groups have several distinct advantages, allowing participants to do the following:

- Share notes, study tips, and ideas.
- Facilitate learning new material and completing class projects.
- Make friends and network.
- Provide experience in working collaboratively.

Being part of a study group is a great way to get more personally involved in your education. A group activity makes you accountable to other people for showing up, contributing, and demonstrating your knowledge. Mixing study with socializing will keep you more alert and engaged. Plus, you gain access to the memories, notes, and ideas of everyone in your study group. Just make sure that your study group stays focused on studying.

How do you form a study group? One way is to organize an online virtual study group whose members don't necessarily live in the same geographic area. The alternative is to get together with fellow students from your class or campus. Whether virtual or face to face, a poorly organized study group can be a frustrating and unproductive experience. To get the most benefits from a study group, try the following:

- Keep the size of your group appropriate to the study goals you have agreed upon.
- Make sure group members are committed to doing the work and meeting on a regular basis.
- Have a rotating chairperson who will call the meeting to order, follow the agenda, and keep the group on task.
- Agree to a start and stop time for each meeting. Have one member serve as the timekeeper.
- Plan an agenda for each meeting; appoint someone to keep the minutes so that everyone in the group has a record of what was accomplished and what the goals are going forward.

Online Resources

As noted earlier, the Internet offers unlimited opportunities to share information through a wide range of formats or platforms.

Wikis. Besides blogs, podcasts, and websites, there is a rapidly growing number of wikis. *Wiki* comes from the Hawaiian term for *fast* or *quick*. In technological terms, a wiki is a webpage that many users can modify, or change. Wikis can be open to the public or password-protected. Users are able to edit documents, add links, delete or insert information, and access earlier versions of the wiki.

Wikis allow collaborative activities to happen online. Each member of the online team is both an author and an editor, contributing ideas

Practice Now: Engaged

An important side benefit to forming a study group is that you create a golden opportunity to practice teamwork skills. Study groups run into high-pressure times when big tests are coming up, creating opportunities for tension and conflict. When you see the bossy side come out of one of your study group mates (or yourself!), see the opportunity to practice engaging with peers.

and information to the group's project. Once you decide to become part of an online collaboration, you need only Internet access and a web browser. No special software or training is necessary. However, if the wiki you're using is limited to authorized users, you will also need a login (user name and password).

Suppose you are preparing for a career as a graphic designer. For your term project, you are working with a team of students on a package of marketing materials for an environmentally conscious home heating company. Your team has decided to use a wiki to supplement face-to-face meetings. You can post design concepts and incorporate feedback from your teammates simply by accessing the wiki. And since the project exists online, you and your team can work on it at any time of the day or night.

Virtual study groups. Meeting in cyberspace is not nearly as intimate as meeting with fellow students face to face, but a virtual study group can provide the pleasure of social interaction and the support that comes with being part of a dedicated group. Some applications, like Windows Live Messenger, integrate instant messaging with social networking. So, while group members are trading class notes, preparing for an exam, or working on a Microsoft PowerPoint presentation, they can also share photos and use their webcams to connect in real time. If you happen to miss an online session, it's not a big deal. A system like Windows Live Messenger automatically archives each session, including discussion threads, notes, drawings, brainstorming, or whatever your group uses. So, all you have to do is log on to see exactly what you missed.

Message board sites like phpBB are also places where you can set up a cyber study space. Let's say you are part of a study group for an electronics course. Your group can create its own message board and decide whether it is public or private. If it is private, then only

authorized users, sharing the same pool of information, can log on to contribute ideas and participate in group discussions.

With the introduction of cloud computing, you no longer have to be tied down to one particular computer. Cloud computing uses distant servers to store all sorts of files so you and the people in your study group can work on the same material no matter where you happen to be. For example, free applications like Google Docs allow users to share a whole range of files, from text documents and PDFs to videos, spreadsheets, and drawings.

> **True**Story
>
> "In my first Web development course, I had trouble creating basic Web pages. I felt like an idiot and thought about dropping out. But a friend pulled me into an online study group. At first, I was afraid other students would think I was dumb. I didn't participate much at first, but everyone in the group was encouraging and supportive. Soon, I felt quite comfortable asking questions, and it helped a lot to get instant feedback. I really like creating Web pages now!"

Community Resources

As you discover and utilize the many resources available to you on campus and online, be sure to find out what community-based programs may also serve your educational needs. A good place to begin your search is the local public library. Public libraries provide educational services to students of all ages. In addition to its collection of documents and books, the library may offer lecture programs, book discussions, film series, art displays, author visits, and meeting rooms. And if you're looking for a quiet place to study, you can't beat a book-lined corner of the public library.

As mentioned earlier, coffee shops are another community resource that can provide a

quiet, but not too quiet, work environment. Your neighborhood coffee shop may be closer to your home than your local library is, and if you can't get away from the distractions at home, coffee shops are a great place to go. In addition to a table to work at and a great cup of coffee to keep you alert, some shops even offer free Internet access. If you don't like studying by yourself, you can always round up the members of your study group and arrange to meet in a coffee shop or some other public place.

Look at your city's website for resources in your area. You may also find that the community center has resources for adult education, and it may be more convenient than your school campus. The center may have listings for classes on effective time management, planning, scheduling, and even studying. Your community is where you spend most of your time, so it is wise to check out the resources you have available to you.

Techniques for Successful Studying

So, you've identified a great place to study. You've got all the materials you need to get down to the business of studying. Your schedule is right there in front of you, and your mental attitude is upbeat. In a word, you're pumped and ready to go. So, what's next? How do you tackle those difficult reading assignments? What techniques can you use to transform the best of intentions into a productive, results-driven study routine?

Set Yourself up for Success

Before you even begin to study, it's important to take the time to set yourself up to succeed.

In other words, make a plan so that studying will be a positive experience with good results. What else do you need to do to set yourself up for success? Make sure to plan so that your time is used effectively.

Be realistic. You have your study schedule in front of you, but take a look and make sure it is realistic. Planning to study for six hours every day sounds like it will help you succeed, but in reality, it will cause you to burn out pretty quickly. Instead, plan short blocks of time for studying. One hour used effectively can produce more results than four hours that are unfocused or disorganized. Effective use of time means that you are motivated, you have what you need, you are paying attention to the material, and you are actively studying. Do plan to take short breaks to maintain energy. But make sure you get back on track after the break!

Prioritize. Look at the priorities on your schedule. Are you trying to do everything? Or are you ignoring important, must-do tasks to make time to study? You must set priorities so that the tasks that *must* get done—such as work, caring for children, paying bills—are not ignored. On the other hand, you can't possibly do everything on your list and make time for effective study. If there are items on your list that can be done another day, such as going to a movie or cleaning out closets, then move them so you can make studying a priority. Remember, it's about balancing your must-dos with your want-to-dos. If you commit to prioritizing, you can make a realistic plan for completing tasks and still have time for optional—and fun—tasks as well.

Use your resources. Finally, make use of the many and varied resources available on campus, online, and in the community. Establish a positive relationship with your instructors, setting aside time to ask questions, and ask for guidance if you have trouble completing an assignment. Make a commitment to solve whatever problems you encounter. For instance, if the textbook you're using doesn't give you the answers you need, search online. Go to the library and track down other sources. If you have a tutor, discuss the problem with him or her. Explore every path or resource that has the potential to help you reach your goal.

Know yourself. A final word about setting yourself up for success: There is no ultimate, perfect set of guidelines for achieving academic success. What works for one person may not work for you. Learning how to study takes a certain amount of trial and error. If you find that

your grades and test scores are improving as a result of practicing good study habits, then take a careful look at how you have been studying. Try to identify those strategies that really made a difference in your academic performance. Conversely, single out any habits or strategies that are keeping you from reaching your goals, and change them for the better.

Use Tried and True Concentration Techniques

If you want your study time to be effective, you have to concentrate on the task, but that is often easier said than done. If you have trouble concentrating or want to improve your ability to concentrate, there are some effective techniques you can use. Having a quiet, distraction-free study environment is helpful, but sometimes you can still have trouble concentrating even when there aren't any distractions.

Reward yourself. Plan to treat yourself to a reward once you've achieved your study goals. Say you've planned to read two chapters and take notes. When you've finished taking notes, and you feel like you understand the material, reward yourself. The reward could be getting a snack, listening to music, going for a walk, chatting with a friend, working on a hobby, playing a video game, or checking your Facebook page. Taking a break can be energizing and give you enough motivation to return to your work.

Vary study time. Remember to switch subjects every few hours to build variety into your study session. Also try changing how you are studying. For instance, if you've been reading a textbook for an hour or so, try working on a writing assignment or doing some online research. To offset fatigue and muscle stiffness, do something physical every hour or so. A brisk, five-minute walk or some vigorous stretching will get your blood going and prepare you for the next chunk of study time.

Bring your attention back. Even when you are using the concentration strategies described above, you may still find it hard to stay focused, especially if you're tired, or the subject matter is boring or difficult, or worries begin to crowd your mind. If worrying is a major distraction, then try setting aside a "worry time" devoted exclusively to going over whatever troubles are weighing on your mind. Then, when it's time to study, you will be more able to focus. Another technique, particularly when your thoughts begin to drift, is to bring yourself back to the present moment. With your eyes open or closed, simply repeat the expression "be here now" until you feel ready to redirect your energy on the work you need to do.

> ## Building **Background**
>
> **Concentration** is actively focusing your attention on one task or handling one task at a time. But in today's busy world, we are often encouraged to multitask, or do many things at once. If your mind wanders or you are listening to a TV show while you are reading, that hour is wasted time. Concentration techniques—strategies you can use to help you focus your mind on what you are doing—can help you make your study time more effective. Think about concentration as a physical skill, much like running. You have to train your brain to focus on what you are doing and filter out what you don't need to pay attention to.

Unit Summary

- Each person has a unique learning style with its own strengths and weaknesses. A commonly used model places learners into three basic categories: visual learners, auditory learners, and kinesthetic learners. Once you've identified your learning style, you can adjust your study routine to take advantage of how you learn best.

- Getting organized is an essential part of preparing for academic success. It includes organizing your study space, stocking up on supplies, and creating a realistic study schedule.

- Maintaining a positive attitude helps you establish priorities and realistic study goals and follow an effective study routine.

- Draw upon a wide range of campus, online, and community resources to help you succeed.

- Setting yourself up for success involves planning a study space and schedule, setting priorities, and taking responsibility for your learning.

- Maintain concentration by using techniques to keep you in the moment as you study.

Important Terms

How well do you know these terms? Look them up in your glossary if you need help remembering them.

distractions	**learning style**	**resources**
prioritize	**attitude**	**concentration**

TO-DO List

✔ Take an inventory of your current stock of study supplies (equipment, materials, etc.). What supplies do you have on hand? What do you still need? What supplies don't you have but still need? Now make an appointment with yourself to get whatever supplies you're lacking.

✔ If you don't already have a functioning study space, now is the time to find one and fix it up to serve your needs. If you study at home, are there any **distractions** you need to consider? For instance, is your study space close to the TV? Do you have loud neighbors? If you have children, how noisy are they? You may decide that studying at home is not an option. In that case, look for a quiet, distraction-free space on or off campus and make sure it will be accessible when you need it.

✔ Review your study schedule and find ways to add in breaks and rewards to lower stress and improve **concentration.** Make a list of rewards you can look forward to and some creative ways to keep yourself motivated.

Exercises

1. Think about prior experiences you've had as a student. Identify study habits that may have been responsible for your not doing well on a test or a paper. Describe those habits in detail. Finally, list what you need to do differently in order to be a successful student.

2. Complete the learning style questionnaire on the Pearson Tutor Center website: www.pearsontutorservices.com/learning_style.html. Click the "Submit" button when you finish. You will then receive an automatic assessment of your preferred learning style. Write a response to the result. Do you agree? Do you disagree? Then make a list of ways you can modify your study habits to more closely reflect your unique learning style.

3. Make a list of resources that are available to you on campus, online, and in your community. You may need to go online and visit your school's website or your city's website. Create a plan for learning more about some of the resources and how they can help you succeed.

4. Create a list that prioritizes all of your responsibilities, including work, family, friends, and fun. Rank each one by importance, and then create a weekly schedule that includes study time, being sure to pay attention to priorities each day. It should be general enough to let you make changes on a weekly or daily basis.

UNIT 10

Test Taking

Practicing ongoing study strategies to avoid having to cram for tests

Preparing for tests academically, mentally, and physically

Using proven test-taking strategies

t he words "test" and "anxiety" are often used together, as in "test-taking anxiety." Most students find tests stressful; some even become physically ill at the prospect of an upcoming test. However, it doesn't have to be that way. Test taking is a skill, and you can improve your performance by learning and practicing the strategies in this unit. It is important to become a confident test taker. Although you probably won't have to take too many tests on the job, you might have to take a certification exam or another high-stakes test at some point in order to achieve your goals. It's time to tackle test taking, so that you will be in control of your results later.

Getting Ready for the Test

What is your test preparation pattern? Are you the Procrastinator, who is convinced there will always be time later on to study and prepare for that quiz or final exam? Do you promise yourself that you will hit the books right after you watch that TV show, or check your email, or make that phone call? Then before you know it, the term is nearly over and you've got only a few days left to prepare for the big test. So you end up doing serious last-minute cramming, with gallons of coffee to keep you going.

Or maybe you're the Stress Case, who can think of nothing else but the next test. You never feel you're prepared enough, no matter how much you study or how hard you try to anticipate the type of questions your instructor will ask. As test time approaches, you become more and more agitated and worried, convinced you'll do poorly and believing your entire life is on the line. Your fears and worries become so intense that they block you from actually testing well.

Obviously, the two profiles described above are extreme examples. But both illustrate a common issue: It is important to prepare for tests in a positive, healthy way. Stressing yourself out by studying nonstop is just as bad as cramming all the material into your head in a few days. The good news is that you don't have to follow either profile. You can use strategies to help you prepare with plenty of time and with low stress and worry.

Maintain Effective Study Strategies

When you know a test is coming up, you might take more detailed notes, or pay closer attention in class, or read your assignments. However, if you made an effort to consistently complete assignments throughout the course, studying for the test would be easier. Why? Because the material you study wouldn't be new—you would have already read it, heard it, and taken notes on it. Instead of separating test preparation from studying, think of studying as a key element of successful test taking. By taking each assignment or academic task seriously, you will be preparing yourself to perform well on tests. The following strategies will not only help you learn, but also help you save time right before the test:

Complete reading assignments on time. Keeping up with reading seems to take a lot of time, but reading actually takes more time if you put it off. When you cram right before a test, you need to take more notes, and you need to go through your textbook inefficiently to look up terms. Also, research shows that spacing learning out over time is more effective than cramming right before the test.[1] When you are given a reading assignment, take the time to complete it. Not just the night before it's due, either. As you've learned in earlier units, make time in your weekly schedule to preview the reading, skimming it for main ideas and details, and then tackle the reading section by section so you can concentrate on what you are reading. Then when you go to class, you'll feel knowledgeable, prepared, and ready to learn more.

Take notes in class. Say you've read the unit and are prepared for class. It can be tempting to sit back and just let the instructor's words wash over you. But what if the instructor points out the important ideas in that unit? Or shares additional information that isn't in the reading assignment? What if the instructor makes a

[1] Kornell, N. (2009). Optimising learning using flashcards: Spacing is more effective than cramming. *Applied Cognitive Psychology, 23*(9), 1297–1317. doi:10.1002/acp.1537

connection to something else? What if *you* make a connection to something else? If you don't take notes, you won't remember that information tomorrow, let alone when you sit down to study for the test. Listen actively and take notes during class so you have something to review before test time.

Organize your study materials. In school, you will acquire information from a variety of sources: textbooks, classroom lectures, study group discussions, tutoring sessions, etc. Since the information is delivered to you in different ways, you may have different kinds of study materials. For example, you may have a notebook with class notes, your textbook with highlighted text and notes in the margin, and digital notes from your study group or journal. And each type of study material will likely have different information. For example, your reading notebook will have notes on main ideas, while your digital notes will include your own ideas or reflections on the topic. Organizing this information—gathering it into one place or at least

making sure it is quickly accessible—is a valuable study strategy and an important part of test preparation. You want to make sure you have everything you need so you don't miss reviewing an important main idea or personal connection.

If you follow the strategies above, you will be very familiar with the material, you will have a lot of study materials to review, and you will be organized and prepared to study for the test. It's important to recognize that a test assesses, or measures, how well you know the topic. Because the test will measure your knowledge about a bigger chunk of material, you can't rely on the same amount of time that you used during regular school assignments. You have to accelerate, or speed up, your study time. Set aside additional time for studying for a test—remembering not to let any other schoolwork slide—and make your study time focused so it is effective. You will read more about how to study for a test effectively later in this unit.

Practice Now: Goal-Oriented

Goal-Oriented students take initiative by asking their instructors what they need to prepare for the test and how the test will be structured. If you feel shy about asking for this information, start practicing now. Some instructors may be annoyed by the questions, but many will give you and your classmates important hints about where to focus in your studying. Others will set up office hours. Students rarely attend office hours, so be one of the ones who arrive and ask questions.

Find Out About the Upcoming Test

What else can you do to prepare for the test? It may seem obvious, but you can find out more about the test. In many cases, the instructor will give you the information below. If not, then ask. Your preparation will be less stressful if you know the following before you begin studying:

Test material. What material will you be asked about? Vocabulary words? A specific set of information, such as conditions that can cause visual impairment or guidelines for maintaining patient confidentiality? An entire unit's worth of information? If you know what will be tested, you can focus the material you study.

Test format. Knowing the format, or style of the test, can help you prepare your answers as you study. Some common formats are essay questions, true-false questions, short-answer questions, fill-in-the-blank questions, multiple-choice questions, and a mix of question types. See Figure 10.1 for a sample of what these question types might look like. Later in this unit we'll look more closely at which test preparation techniques to use with specific test formats.

You can also study graded exams that you've already taken that test similar topics. These can serve as useful models that will show you the types of questions you will likely encounter and the range of material you will be expected to know. During the weeks leading up to the test, pay close attention to what your instructor says in class. He or she might give clues about the upcoming test, such as emphasizing certain terms or concepts by writing them on the board or including them on a handout. The material the instructor chooses to highlight may very well indicate what information will appear on the test.

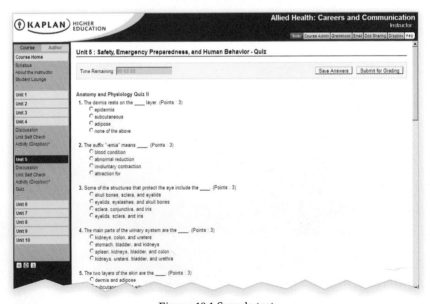

Figure 10.1 Sample test

Use Effective Test-Prep Strategies

In order to review your study materials as efficiently and effectively as possible, you'll need to create a study schedule. Let's assume you have already drawn up a schedule that includes your responsibilities (going to work, picking up the kids, attending classes, exercising) and your free time (relaxing, seeing family, socializing, etc.). You don't need to scratch this plan and start over. But you do need to modify it to be sure you have set aside enough time to prepare for your exam. So, sit down with your study schedule and figure out when you can put in the extra time to prepare for an upcoming test.

Begin your preparation at least a week or two before the test. You may need to start even earlier if you are preparing for a major certification exam. Starting early is critical—you will do better on the test if you study one hour each day for ten days than if you study five hours each day for two days.

Once you have a plan, you are now ready to review the study materials you've organized. In addition to reviewing your class notes, review assigned readings and journals from your digital sessions. Your journal entries can give you an insightful overview of the course. You may ask yourself, "Where do I begin? Which notebook or handout should I pick up first and start to review?" An effective way to begin your review is to organize your notes and other study materials by creating **master lists,** or information organized into categories. Here are some general list categories:

Key terms. These are important words or phrases that are used again and again in the subject, often found in a glossary.

Themes. These are the main ideas, or the most important ideas, of a concept or topic of study.

Related concepts. These are ideas that are connected to other ideas. Related concepts are not as obvious as major themes; instead, they are details that support the major themes.

You may use these categories, or you may decide to create your own. The important thing to remember is to group information so that it is not overwhelming and so that it has an order you can follow as you study.

But even with well-organized notes, you still have to make sure you understand and can recall information. Use the following study aids and techniques to improve your ability to understand and retain what you need to know for an upcoming test.

Flash cards. Classic flash cards are simply 3 × 5 or 4 × 6 index cards that you can use for a variety of learning purposes. Suppose you're studying to become a certified nursing assistant and you need to know how to administer CPR (cardiopulmonary resuscitation). This

procedure involves a sequence of steps. Missing a step or performing the steps in the wrong order could endanger someone's life. Using flash cards, write each step on a separate card. Shuffle the cards so the steps are out of order. Try to put the cards (and the steps) in the correct order. You can repeat this as many times as you need.

You can also use flash cards when you're trying to remember key terms or concepts. Write one term on one side of a card. Write the correct definition on the reverse side. Do this for all the terms you need to know for the exam. Using the cards, test yourself by first looking at a term and then saying it aloud or writing its definition. Turn the card over to see how you did. Invite a friend, study partner, or relative to quiz you.

For concepts, ideas, or themes, come up with questions you think your instructor might ask on the test. Write each question on one side of a flash card and a detailed answer on the reverse side of the card. Use the cards to test your understanding and ability to recall.

CPR
Call 911
Tilt head, lift chin, check breathing
Give 2 breaths
Position hands on center of chest
Push firmly 2 inches 30 times
Repeat until help arrives

cardiopulmonary resuscitation

One advantage of flash cards is that you can carry them with you and use them whenever you have some free time. Say you're waiting to have your hair cut or to see the doctor. Just take out your flash cards and get to work! They are great tools to have and to use as you review your course materials.

In your digital classroom, you will find digital flashcards that have already been prepared for some topics. These flashcards may also be compatible with your mobile device, so you can practice on the go, as with classic flashcards. You may also be able to find free digital flashcards on the Internet for some common topics.

Memorization techniques. Memorization techniques are another invaluable aid to helping you prepare for a test. These techniques are also called **mnemonic devices.** You're probably already familiar with some mnemonic devices. Basically, these devices use letters, images, sounds, or rhymes as memory boosters. They are shorthand ways of locking in "must-know" information and making it relatively easy to recall. You can use mnemonic devices for all sorts of information, from key terms to important concepts. As you get ready to take the test and begin by reviewing your notes and assignments, determine which elements or details you need to remember. Then use a mnemonic device or study aid to help you lock this information into your memory.

Here are some examples of memorization aids, or mnemonic devices:

- Expression mnemonics are the most popular mnemonic devices. Expression mnemonics are made up phrases or sentences using the first letter of each word you want to remember. Have you ever tried to recall the planets in order from the sun? Use an expression mnemonic: **M**y **V**ery **E**ager **M**other **J**ust **S**erved **U**s **N**uts (Mercury, Venus, Earth, Mars, Jupiter, Saturn, Uranus, Neptune). These expressions are helpful when you need to remember words in a specific order; just write the first letter of each word in the order you need to remember it, and then create a funny phrase.

- Acronyms are similar to expression mnemonics except the first letter of each word is used to make one word, not a sentence. For example, the acronym PEMDAS stands for the sequence of mathematical operations to be used when solving math problems: **P**arentheses, **E**xponents, **M**ultiplication, **D**ivision, **A**ddition, and **S**ubtraction. By remembering this made-up word, a math student will also remember the order of operations.
- Name acronyms use the first letter of each word in a list of words to make up a name. For example, *ROY G. BIV* helps you remember the order of colors in a rainbow: **R**ed, **O**range, **Y**ellow, **G**reen, **B**lue, **I**ndigo, **V**iolet.
- Rhymes, poems, and songs can help you remember key concepts or ideas. Often, the brain can recall words better if they are set to a tune or if they rhyme. For example, to remember how many days are in each month, many rely on this rhyme: *Thirty days have September, April, June, and November. Of twenty-eight there is but one, and all the rest have thirty-one*. Try putting a concept into a rhyme or a song with a catchy tune.
- Chaining can help you remember a list or a sequence of events. With chaining, you make up a simple story that uses key words. For example, the steps for CPR are 1) call for help; 2) push the chest; 3) blow breath into the mouth. You could use this chain: *I will call my mother and tell her I need to pump up my tire before I blow my top.*

Visualization. The previous study aid examples are all associated with words, but you can also use drawings and visualization to help you recall information. For example, if you have a list of words to remember, you can draw a picture that illustrates all the words. When you take the test, you can visualize the picture.

People. Other people are some of the best resources, outside of your own notes, that you can use as you prepare for a test. Start with your instructor. Arrange an appointment to discuss ideas or concepts you need to review. Before the meeting, prepare the questions you want to ask or list ideas you want clarified. If a face-to-face appointment isn't possible, then an email exchange with your instructor might do the trick. If you belong to a study group, consult with the other members of your group. Do you have a tutor? Arrange to meet with him or her for some one-on-one guidance. And if you are having trouble understanding the assigned reading selections or can't find information you need, a librarian can help you find additional texts on the test topic in the library.

Prep yourself. Finally, examine your approach to taking a test. Since you aren't writing the test, and since you won't know exactly what questions will be asked, it may seem as if all you can do is wait until test day and see how it goes. Many students tend to think that a test is something that will happen to them, that they either know it or they don't, and that there's nothing they can do in order to prepare. But if you prepare for the test, you do have control over what information or knowledge you have learned. Take an active role by writing down five key things that you have learned and that you want your instructor to know you have learned. Then, as you are taking the test, look for a place where you can insert those five concepts. You can take control of the test by making sure you show your instructor what you know.

Taking the Test

After weeks of intense rehearsing, actors in the theater finally have to perform in front of an actual audience. In some ways, you are faced with a similar challenge. The time is nearing when you will have to put down your notes and take the test for which you've been preparing.

Take Care of Yourself

As the day of the test draws near, the last thing you'll want is to be bleary-eyed from lack of sleep, your mind overflowing with information, and your heart racing with anxiety and too much caffeine. A better plan is to show up at the test feeling calm, relaxed, and prepared. Take good care of yourself. Get a good night's sleep before the test. You can do a final read-through of your notes, but avoid trying to memorize new information at the last minute. Be sure to arrive early at the test site with all the materials you need, such as pens and pencils or even a calculator or laptop computer, if

appropriate. If the instructor doesn't mind your eating during the test, pack some high-energy snacks to give you that needed energy and help you stay focused. Choose your seat carefully. Avoid sitting close to anything or anyone you think will distract you as you take the test. And be sure you can easily keep track of the time with a watch, a wall clock, or another device. (Be careful not to use your phone as your time-keeper, since you could appear to be texting or cheating in some other way.) Chances are that the test will be divided into sections, so you'll want to be able to allot enough time to each section—and, of course, to finish the test on time. If you find yourself becoming stressed out, try a **relaxation exercise,** which is an activity that helps you relax, regain calm, and reduce stress. Examples of relaxation exercises include stretching, closing your eyes and visualizing a peaceful place, and practicing deep breathing. If possible, take a short break to lower your stress level and restore your energy.

Type of Test Question	Strategy
True-False: Determine if a statement is true (can be proven as fact) or false (cannot be proven as fact).	• If any part of the statement is false, then the entire statement is false. • The entire statement or sentence must be true in order to qualify as the right answer.
Multiple choice: Choose the best possible answer from a list of 3–5 choices.	• Eliminate choices that are completely or partly false. • The answer that seems best at first may not be the correct one. • Eliminate choices that seem unrelated to the test question.

Figure 10.2 Test question strategies

Use Effective Test-Taking Strategies

Picture yourself at the test site. You're rested, you've got what you need, and you feel prepared to do your best. The instructor passes out the test. Now what? Just as there are strategies to prepare for the test, there are strategies to take the test. Approach the test with the following steps:

- If you are taking a paper-based test, quickly look through the entire test before you begin. Knowing how the test is organized can help you plan your time. Some questions take longer to answer than others. Write down the time when you plan to finish each section. This will help you move on if one section is taking too much time. If you are taking your test digitally, you may not have the option of looking forward; just do the best you can to plan, using the information that you can acquire.
- Read the directions for each section carefully. Make sure you understand what you need to do before you begin. Rushing through instructions is a common error that can have unhappy consequences!
- Read each question carefully so you understand exactly what is being asked.

- If you are unsure of an answer, move on to the next question. Make sure to leave time to go back to skipped questions, though.
- Look for clues to the answer in the question itself.
- Watch the time so you can pace yourself against your time plan. You don't want to spend too much time on one question and then run out of time for other questions.
- If you finish early, go back and check to be sure you have answered every question and entered the answers correctly. Do not spend too much time second-guessing your answers. It is a common problem for students to become anxious and start to doubt their answers. If you find yourself changing a lot of answers, slow down—it is a common error for anxious students to change correct answers to incorrect answers.

The previous list includes general strategies for all tests. However, different types of questions require different test-taking strategies. The chart below lists approaches you can follow with two common types of test questions: multiple choice and true-false.

For both true-false and multiple-choice questions, watch for qualifiers, or words that change the sense or meaning of a sentence. For instance, "It always rains in Seattle" is not the same as "It often rains in Seattle." The first sentence is false because it has the word *always*. The second sentence, however, is true. The words *always* and *often* are qualifiers. Qualifiers can make the difference between a correct option and an incorrect choice.

And what do you do if you've followed all of the strategies and you still aren't sure which answer to choose? Practice **intelligent guessing.** Also called making an educated guess, intelligent guessing is not just choosing blindly. Instead, you first eliminate answer choices you know to be wrong or misleading. Obviously, it is best to eliminate as many choices as you can. Then you carefully consider the remaining choices. Choose the one that is the most right, or the one that "sounds" right to you. Trust the knowledge you've gained to make an intelligent guess.

Tackle Essays on Exams

Essay questions are very different from other types of test questions. **Essays** are written responses to a question that are at least one paragraph. Essay questions ask you to write a paragraph or more to respond to the question. Not only do you not have answer choices to eliminate, you have to write a long response.

When it comes to answering essay questions, consider using the following strategies:

- As with other types of tests, read the directions carefully. The directions may contain hints that will help you formulate your answer.

- If given a choice of essay topics, choose the topic you can address most effectively or the one that will best let you demonstrate to your instructor how much you've learned. If you have prepared five things you know and want to convey to your instructor, the essay question is a great place to include some of them.

- Read the essay question carefully to make sure you understand what is expected in your answer. Often, the essay question asks for a specific format ("Write a paragraph" or "Write a sentence") and can have multiple parts ("Explain how the central nervous system functions and what happens when parts of the system are injured."). Be sure to follow the specific instructions.

- Try to connect the essay topic to one or more of the themes presented during the course. Remember that the test covers what you've already learned, not new material, and take advantage of what you already know.

- Before beginning to write your essay, make notes on the key points, terms, and concepts you want to cover. Create an outline of the main ideas to plan the order of each concept or point. Write your time plan next to your outline, so you can avoid spending too much time on one section of your essay.

- Decide how you want to structure or organize your essay. A standard way of organizing an essay is the **three-part structure:** introduction, body, and conclusion. If that doesn't seem to fit the essay question, you can organize it by sequence/time, compare/contrast, or main idea and details.

Organization/Structure	Explanation
Three-part structure	• Introduction • Body • Conclusion
Sequence/time	Information is given in the order events happen or in time order.
Compare/contrast	• Explain how things or concepts are similar. • Explain how things or concepts are different.
Main idea and details	List main idea and details that support it: • Main idea • Detail 1 • Detail 2 • Detail 3

Figure 10.3 Essay question organization/structure

After the Test: Follow-Up Suggestions

So, you've completed the test and received your grade. Now you can put the entire experience behind you and forget about it, right? Well, you can do that. But then you'll just have to go through the same experience for the next test. And what if your test score surprised you? A better option is to take some time to reflect on your test preparation and how it affected your grade. It's not hard to do. Taking a few minutes to write down some notes before you forget the test will benefit you down the road as you prepare for future tests.

Turn the Exam into a Learning Experience

Once your instructor has graded the test and given it back to you, take time to look at the test. Identify the errors you made. Can you see a pattern in these errors? Were most of your errors related to factual information, for instance, or to larger themes and concepts? Can you spot any errors that have more to do with misunderstanding or not following directions? Or did you misread test questions and choose incorrect answers as a result? This kind of careful review can provide you with valuable information about your performance on the test.

For example, if you made errors because you skipped reading directions, then you know to read directions carefully during your next test. Or if most of your errors were related to not understanding a concept, you can schedule time to talk to your instructor before the next test to make sure you understand the main ideas well.

Speaking of talking with your instructor, you can also review your test with your instructor. Ask for suggestions on strategies or steps you can take to improve your score on the next test. Your instructor can also help you understand why you got certain questions wrong or why your essay received a low score.

And if you did well on the test, pat yourself on the back for a job well done. Then, be sure to review the test anyway. Take the time to think about what you did to prepare that may have helped you succeed. Did you make more time to study? Did you take advantage of a study group or use a mnemonic device? If you identify strategies that helped you do well, you can use them again. No matter how you scored, save your tests and quizzes so that you can use them to help you prepare for the next exam.

Take Time to Relax

Once the test is over, and you've taken a few moments to reflect and organize the material, give yourself a break. Playing the "what if" game won't change the result, and if you've taken steps to learn from your test-taking experience, you can apply new strategies to the next exam. If you find that you can't stop replaying things in your mind, find something fun that will distract you. Check out that band your friends have been raving about. Get in some workout time at the gym. Do something that will make you feel good about yourself

TrueStory

"In college, I had a really easy English class and a really hard math class. Since I was a good writer, I didn't pay much attention during English and sat in the back of the class cramming for math. Well, one day, my instructor said to read a unit of the book for an in-class essay. Since I wasn't paying attention, I misheard what she said and read the wrong unit! The in-class essay was a one-hour nightmare. I had to spend the rest of the term convincing my teacher that I wasn't an idiot."

and restore your energy so you're ready to get back to your studies. Plan to get together with friends or family. Treat yourself to a reward for having done your best, such as a watching a movie, going out with friends, or even staying home to really relax. It is important to plan some down time, just as you planned your study time.

Maintain a Confident Attitude

If you did well on the test, congratulate yourself. Better yet, celebrate! If you didn't do as well as you expected, try to frame your performance as a learning experience. Do your best to maintain a confident attitude. And why shouldn't you feel confident and hopeful? You're making sacrifices to invest in your education so you can have a more rewarding career and build your future. You're successfully balancing your classes with outside interests, family life, and perhaps even a job. That's plenty, and you should be proud and confident.

Most of all, remember to keep the test in perspective. In other words, remember that one test is only a small part of your academic life. If you look at the "big picture," which is your life as a whole, you'll see that how you did on one test isn't the most important thing in your life. You know what the test-taking experience is like, and you now have the tools you need to succeed. You know how to get ready for a test and how to take a test. Just as importantly, you have the ability to turn a test into a learning experience that can only increase your chances of success.

ON THE **JOB**

Sylvia had just finished her program studying to be an ultrasound technician. She knew she was lucky because she worked at a doctor's office and could ask the ultrasound techs questions as she studied for her certification exam. The day of the test, she was really nervous, but she knew she'd prepared as well as she could. Sylvia was shocked when she learned that she hadn't passed the exam. "I think I'll just be a receptionist, then," she miserably told Amy, an ultrasound tech at her office.

Amy laughed. "I failed my first test, too. It's not the end of the world. It's just one test. You've worked hard. You should try again. I can quiz you over lunch breaks if that will help." Sylvia felt better, and the next week, she set up a quiz schedule with Amy and applied to take the test again.

Unit Summary

- You can take some of the anxiety out of test taking by keeping up with studies from day one: taking and reviewing class notes, completing reading assignments, and drawing upon available resources whenever you feel the need for additional support.

- Think of your test prep as extra study time you need to build into your study schedule. Plan to prepare for the test in shorter study sessions over longer periods of time.

- Gather and organize all the materials you'll need to review. Consider drawing up a master list of key terms and concepts from the course. Then group your materials according to this list.

- Find out what you're being tested on and what sort of test format your instructor will be using. This is very important information, as it will help you focus on what you absolutely must master for the test. Prepare what you plan to say on the test—show what you know.

- On the day of the test, use a systematic approach to taking the test. Before you begin, take a minute or so to look over the test to see how it is set up. Read all directions carefully. Know precisely what each question is asking. Budget your time for each section.

- When the test is over, use it as a learning experience, and then take a break. You deserve it.

TO-DO List

1. Create a test prep study schedule for any upcoming test(s). This can be a separate schedule or part of your regular study schedule. Estimate how much time you will need based on some or all of the following factors:
   - ✔ How well you've been keeping up with your studies
   - ✔ How well you understand the course content
   - ✔ How much material you will need to review
   - ✔ The type of test you're preparing for

2. Practice writing an **essay.** First, brainstorm a short list of possible topics that interest you and that you know something about. Give yourself a time limit (10 or 15 minutes), review this unit's essay-writing strategies, and then start writing. When you finish, ask friends to read over your essay and give you some feedback. As a final step, you could use this feedback to revise your essay.

3. Reward yourself! Being a successful student demands hard work, especially when you're getting ready for a test. Make a list of rewards—enjoyable activities or treats for when you've completed your test preparation and have taken the test. You could list your top ten rewards, or even prioritize them. The main thing is to take a break and do something you really enjoy doing.

Important Terms

How well do you know these terms? Look them up in the glossary if you need help remembering them.

master lists   **intelligent guessing**

mnemonic devices   **essays**

relaxation exercises   **three-part structure**

Exercises

1. Find a partner, and take turns interviewing each other about previous test-taking experiences. Use these questions to help you structure the interview: What sorts of tests do you tend to do well on? (Multiple-choice, true-false, essay questions?) What strategies do you use in order to prepare for a test? Which ones have been the most effective? Least effective? Is there anything you need to do better in order to improve your test scores? If so, what is it?

2. Working with a partner, on your own, or in a small group, identify a major topic in one of your courses that you are likely to be tested on. Now break this topic down into key concepts or main ideas. Using index cards as flash cards, write each concept or main idea on one side of a card and the definition or explanation on the opposite side. If you have a partner or are part of a study group, exchange flash cards and test each other. Then consider which areas you didn't cover or still need to work on. Include these on new flash cards.

3. Test your memory! Make up a list of seven to ten key terms from one of your courses. Write them down on a sheet of paper. Create a mnemonic device to help you recall each item on your list. Now exchange your list with a partner or with members of your study group, and test each other's ability to recall the items on each of your lists. To simulate an actual test, make this a timed exercise with "time" called after three minutes. How well did the mnemonic device aid your memory?

Credits

Glossary

academic strategy   a method or plan that helps students succeed in school

action plan   a step-by-step outline of manageable tasks to be completed over a certain time frame in order to reach a goal

active listening   the act of making a conscious effort to hear and comprehend others in conversation

annotating   a note-taking method where notes and questions about the text are written directly in the text, on a separate sheet of paper, or with a digital tool

attitude   your personal view on things

audience   a group to whom you deliver a presentation, or the intended readership for a written document

bias   a preference or inclination that prevents impartial judgment

blog   short for *weblog;* a personal website that combines the functionality of a daily diary with the ability to post photos and videos online; usually offered in a fixed template

business plan   a document that identifies a company's objectives, explains the reasoning behind those objectives, lists the tasks necessary to achieve those goals, and outlines the strategic plan for completing the tasks

casual register   a style of writing or speaking that includes playful language, coined (made-up) words, and incomplete sentences

charting   recording information in chronological order about the progress of a person or situation over a period of time

chronic stress   the body's response to perceived threats, resulting in the body remaining in a continuous state of tension; over time, can lead to physical and psychological illnesses

collaboration   a method of working together with others to achieve a common goal

concentration   the act of actively focusing your attention on something or of handling one task at a time

conflict resolution   the process of ending or minimizing disagreement among groups or individuals, with an emphasis on negotiating to create solutions that take into account the underlying interests and needs of all parties involved

consensus   a decision agreed upon by most of the people concerned

constructive criticism   a well-meant evaluation, intended to help a person improve some aspect of his or her performance

cursor   on a computer screen, the marker that you move with a mouse or trackpad

discussion board   a forum on the Internet where users interested in a common topic can post information, ask questions, and ask for and give feedback

distraction   something that takes away your attention or focus

diversity   a range of differences

essay question   a test question that asks you to write a paragraph or more to respond to the question

expository   describes writing that explains something or teaches how to do something

external reward   a tangible form of recognition, such as money or a prize

formal register   a style of writing or speaking that includes specific, purposeful word choices and complete sentences of varied lengths and structures

function   the purpose for which something is designed, or the action for which a person's role is identified

goal   a specific, measurable objective that can be achieved through your own actions

graphic organizer   a visual tool, such as a chart, that helps you organize your thoughts and notes when reading or learning new information

hard drive   a device that stores data in a computer

hard obligation   a task or commitment with a specific time frame or deadline

hardware   the physical parts of a computer

input port   a type of outlet in a computer, used to attach peripherals

intelligent guessing   the act of eliminating any answer choices you know to be wrong or misleading and choosing the best answer from the remaining choices; also called *making an educated guess*

intermediate goal   an important objective that is achieved over the course of one to three years; usually supports a long-term goal

internal reward   a positive feeling such as satisfaction, happiness, or fulfillment

Internet   a worldwide network composed of smaller, connected computer networks and other computer organizations

keyboard   a panel, usually flat, used for typing letters, numbers, and commands on a computer

learning style   the way in which a person processes information and integrates, or combines, new information with old information

long-term goal   a significant objective that is achieved over a long period of time

main idea   the most important piece of information the author wants to convey about the topic; details are included that support the main idea by telling who, what, when, where, or why

marginalia   notes written in the margin of a text

master list   a list that organizes information you need to recall into categories

mind mapping   a note-taking method that visually links ideas by relationship, with the main idea in the center and the supporting ideas branching out from the main idea

minutes   an official record of what was said and done in a meeting

mnemonic device   a memory technique that takes a word, idea, or concept, and then uses letters, images, sounds, or rhymes to aid recall

monitor   a device that receives information from a computer and displays it on a screen

motivation   something that provides incentive to act

mouse   a handheld device used to move a pointer or a cursor on a computer screen and to send commands to the computer

multiple-choice question   a question that asks you to choose the best possible answer from a list of choices

narrative   a story that describes what happened in detail

negative stress   a lack of pressure or a low-pressure situation that causes performance to decrease

network card   a device that allows a computer to connect to other computers and to the Internet

optical drive   a device in a computer that reads DVDs and CDs

optimum stress   the level of stress that results in peak performance

outline   a graphic organizer that uses Roman and Arabic numerals and upper- and lowercase letters to arrange ideas, details, and examples

outlining   a method of note taking in which information is listed in a hierarchical order, using Roman and Arabic numerals and upper- and lowercase letters

peripheral   an external device that cooperates with a computer

persuasion   influence on a person's values, beliefs, attitudes, or behaviors

portable drive   an external device that stores and transfers digital data

positive stress   pressure that causes an individual's performance to improve

pre-reading   describes strategies used before reading to plan the reading and to prepare yourself to comprehend and remember the text

prioritize   to list things in order of how important they are so that higher-priority tasks get taken care of before lower-priority ones

priority   the level of importance of a task

problem solving   a mental process for moving from a present situation toward a goal

processor   a device that receives, calculates, manipulates, and resolves most of a computer's data; also called a central processing unit (CPU)

procrastination   the act of putting off one activity by turning to other activities

progress notes   a record of information about the progress, or changes, in a person or situation over a period of time

pyramid notes   a top-to-bottom method of note taking that creates a visual pyramid that breaks down the subject, main idea, and supporting details

RAM (random access memory)   memory that programs use while running on a computer

relaxation exercises   activities that help you relax, regain calm, and reduce stress

resource   a source of help

scaffolding   a strategy that uses what you already know as a supporting framework upon which you can build or attach new information

scanning   reading with a wide-angle lens to find a specific piece of information very quickly

shift notes   information about situations that is recorded by the current worker on a shift for the next worker who takes over the job

short-term goal   an objective that is achieved in a short period of time; usually supports long-term and intermediate goals

skimming   quickly running your eyes across the whole text, line by line, to get a sense of the organization of the text and the way the subject is explained

SMART goal   an objective that is specific, measurable, attainable, realistic, and timely

soft obligation   a task or commitment without a specific time frame or deadline

software   the programs and operating systems that are used on a computer; also called applications

Standard American English   the standard or agreed-upon conventions, or rules, of English grammar, including punctuation, capitalization, sentence structure, and spelling

strategy   a careful and deliberate plan or method

strength   an ability developed or mastered through practice and work

strengths diversity   variety in the assets and competencies that people offer

stress   the response of the body to a perceived threat or danger (stressor)

stressor   a perceived threat or danger that triggers the body's stress response

summarizing   the act of using your own words to express your understanding of a topic

summary   a shorter restatement that contains the most important ideas

support system   a social network that helps a person achieve his or her goals

talent   a natural capability

task list   a list of all the tasks an individual needs to accomplish in the day

TCP/IP   a set of communication conventions used by networks connected by the Internet

three-part structure   a typical organization or structure of writing that uses an introduction, a body, and a conclusion

trackpad   a rectangular, touch-sensitive keyboard panel used to move a pointer or cursor on a computer screen and to send commands to the computer

true-false question   a question that asks you to determine if a statement is true (can be proven as fact) or false (cannot be proven as fact)

value   one of a set of guiding principles for a group (such as a company) or an individual

verbatim   in exactly the same wording, or word for word

voice   writing that "speaks" naturally on the page

wiki   an online tool that allows multiple users to post, share, and comment on information

writing to entertain   writing that gives readers enjoyment

writing to inform   writing that teaches or educates readers on a specific topic

writing to persuade   writing that convinces readers to agree with the writer's viewpoint

Index

W